PAUL SELIGSON
TOM ABRAHAM
CRIS GONTOW

English ID

2nd edition

Workbook 2

 Richmond

ID Language map

Question syllabus			Vocabulary	Grammar	Speaking & Skills
1	**1.1**	What's really important in life?	Life priorities	Review of present tenses & simple past	Talk about life priorities
	1.2	Which sense do you use the most?	The senses + sense verbs & adjectives		Talk about sensations & experiences
	1.3	Do you read, hear, or watch a lot of ads?		*Will / won't* for predictions / unplanned decisions	Make predictions
	1.4	What shouldn't you do to stay healthy?	Common illnesses	*Should / shouldn't* for advice	Give advice
	1.5	When do you ask for help?	Expressions for offering, accepting & refusing help		Offer and accept / refuse help
2	**2.1**	Do you ever read newspapers?	News media Genres of news stories		Talk about how you get your news Summarize a news survey
	2.2	What were you doing at 8 o'clock last night?		Past continuous State vs. action verbs	Talk about events
	2.3	What's the world's most serious problem?	Global problems Natural phenomena		Talk about the weather & natural phenomena
	2.4	Was your mom living here when you were born?		Past continuous vs. simple past	Talk about dramatic interruptions
	2.5	What do you carry in your pockets?			Understand or retell a story
3	**3.1**	How often do you travel?	Traveling		Share travel experiences
	3.2	Have you ever been to another country?		Present perfect 1: past experiences	Talk about past experiences
	3.3	Have you sung a song in English yet?		Present perfect 2: completed actions (*already, just, yet*)	Take part in a research project
	3.4	How long have you lived here?	Points & periods in time	Present perfect 3: unfinished past (*for, since*)	Talk about unfinished events
	3.5	Are you a logical person?	Suffixes *-ic, -ment, -al, -ion*		React to unexpected information
4	**4.1**	Were you spoiled as a child?	Personality adjectives		Talk about the kind of child you were
	4.2	What did you use to do as a child?		*Used to* and simple past	Talk about childhood habits & memories
	4.3	Has your taste in music changed?	Ways of listening to music	Past simple vs. *Used to*	Talk about how you listen to music
	4.4	Do you speak English as often as possible?	Adjectives	Comparatives / superlatives / *as... as...*	Make comparisons
	4.5	How many pets have you had?		*So / but*	Talk about pets
5	**5.1**	What would you like to study?	School subjects & facilities		Talk about school subjects Talk about your school & plans
	5.2	What do you have to do tonight?	Class activities	Obligation & prohibition	Talk about class activities Talk about rules
	5.3	Are you a good student?	Good study habits	*Too / enough / too much / too many*	Give tips about school
	5.4	What will you do when you pass this course?		Zero & first conditional	Give advice about traveling
	5.5	How do you usually get in touch?	Ways of communicating	Pronouns & referencing	Warnings & promises phrases

		Question syllabus	Vocabulary	Grammar	Speaking & Skills
6	**6.1**	Have you ever been to Florida?	Leisure time activities	*Go* gerund (verb + -*ing*)	Talk about leisure time activities Talk about a vacation in Florida
	6.2	Would you like to try hang gliding?	Verbs of movement	Prepositions Compound nouns	Talk about how you feel about adventurous sports
	6.3	Do you feel like going out tonight?	Prepositions of movement		Complete two descriptions
	6.4	What do you enjoy doing on your birthday?	Sports vocabulary Phrasal verbs	Verb + infinitive / gerund	Describe how to play a sport
	6.5	Would you rather stay in or go out?	Phrases to express preferences	*would rather*	Make decisions
7	**7.1**	How often do you go to the movies?	Movie vocabulary		Write a movie review
	7.2	Are you crazy about music?	Passionate interests	Pronouns *some-, any-, every-, no-*	Describe a birthday
	7.3	What do you have a lot of at home?		*So & such*	Talk about world records Talk about unusual collections
	7.4	Who was Instagram created by?	Numbers	Passive voice – present & past	Talk about movies
	7.5	Are you a good singer?	Agreeing / disagreeing		Give opinions
8	**8.1**	Are you into science fiction?	Technology	*At / in / on*	Talk about technology
	8.2	Do you ever switch off from technology?	Phrasal verbs	Phrasal verbs	Give instructions about using an app
	8.3	Will space vacations be popular soon?		Future forms 1	Compare predictions about life in the future
	8.4	Is technology making us more, or less, social?	False cognates	Future forms 2	Talk about the future
	8.5	Who do you talk to when you need help?	Signs of the Zodiac	Reduced sentences	Make fortune-telling predictions
9	**9.1**	What do you think of marriage?	Wedding words		Compare weddings Talk about marriage & weddings
	9.2	Do you think romantic movies are entertaining?	Intensifiers	-*ed* & -*ing* adjectives	Express feelings
	9.3	If you had three wishes, what would they be?		Second conditional	Talk about unreal situations
	9.4	Have you ever performed for an audience?	Performers	*May, might, could, must, can't + be*	Make conclusions
	9.5	How do you get on with your siblings?		Pronouns	Talk about siblings
10	**10.1**	Do you often feel stressed?	Causes & symptoms of stress *over / under*		Talk about stress
	10.2	Would you like to change anything in your life?	Lifestyle changes	*less / more / quit* Relative pronouns: *that & who*	Talk about lifestyle changes
	10.3	What's your attitude to money?	Money Alternative lifestyles		Talk about ways to get rich
	10.4	How often do you post on social media?		Questions review *How* + adjective / adverb	Answer a quiz
	10.5	Do you enjoy reading in English?		*one / ones*	Read faster

Audioscript p. 54   Answer Key p. 60   Phrase Bank p. 66   Word List p. 70

1.1 What's really important in life?

1 ▶1.1 **Listen and answer. Follow the model. Write or record your answers.**

Model: *What's your full name?*
Student: *My name's...*
Model: *How do you spell your last name?*

2 **Complete quotes a–f with one of these life priorities. Check the one you like best.**

| career | education | family |
| free time | friends | have fun | love |

a "If you think _____ is expensive, try ignorance!"
Andy McIntyre

b "_____ is when the other person's happiness is more important than your own." H. Jackson Brown Jr.

c "Communication—the human connection—is the key to personal and _____ success."
Paul J. Meyer

d "When you _____ you can do amazing things."
Joe Namath

e "Too much _____ on your hands just leads to trouble." K. Jeffrey Miller

f "You can choose your _____ but you sure can't choose your _____." Harper Lee

3 **Match these priorities to the evening course ad titles a–d.**

☐ fitness ☐ culture
☐ financial security ☐ health

a ART HISTORY

b Do you want to get in shape?

c *Healthy cooking for less money*

d Manage your money

4 **Match titles a–d from 3 to these ads.**

☐ Our exciting evening Zumba class fuses fitness fun with hypnotic Latin rhythms! Any fitness level. Complete beginners welcome.
One week free for 50+

☐ Learn how to prepare dishes that are good for you and don't cost much. Cook 12 dishes over the four-week course, each with a different healthy ingredient. Ingredients are not included.

☐ Would you like to know more about European movements of the 19th and 20th centuries? This course introduces art from the Impressionists to Cubism, exploring painting, sculpture and architecture. Please bring a pen and a notepad.

☐ Are you frustrated by your finances? We can help. Our four-week free course tells you everything you need to know about saving and spending. Thursdays, 7–9 p.m.

5 **Choose the correct option.**

a Yesterday we **cooked / cook** a healthy pizza and I **take / took** it home for dinner.

b Last night we **watched / watch** a presentation about 19th Century architecture.

c At the moment we **learn / 're learning** how to make risotto.

d I **'m wanting / want** to learn how to save more money. That's why I **chose / choose** this course.

e Don't worry, this course **doesn't cost / isn't costing** anything.

f We **meet / 're meeting** every week and it's great fun. I love dancing!

g I **love / 'm loving** this type of art so I **really enjoy / 'm really enjoying** this course.

h I **'m going / went** to the first class last night. It was good but I **'m / was** very tired today!

6 **Match statements a–h in 5 to the four ads in 4.**

7 🎤 **Make it personal** **What's important to you? Record your own "Life in 10 seconds" and email it to a friend or your teacher.**

4

1.2 Which sense do you use the most?

1 Complete the conversations with the pairs of adjectives in the box.

awesome / soft   great / bland   fantastic / awful   sour / spicy

1 A: This food smells _____ .
   B: I agree, but it tastes a little _____ .
2 A: Your sweater looks _____ .
   B: Thank you. The material feels so _____ and lovely.
3 A: What did you think of the band? I thought they sounded _____ .
   B: Really? I thought they sounded _____ ! I have a headache now.
4 A: Is there anything you don't like?
   B: Well, I don't like anything that tastes too _____ or anything too _____ .

2 ▶1.2 Complete ads a–d with the words above the photos. Listen to check.

look at   see   touch   watch

a _____ this awesome offer! This new _____ -screen laptop for only $300. You can use it for work or study, then take off the keyboard and _____ movies and play games when you travel, and use it like a tablet. Come and _____ this and other great prices at Tony's Technology Store. Tony's Tech **store**. Fantastic new laptops and **more**!

eat   smell   smells   taste   tastes

b Breathe through your nose. Can you _____ our fresh bread? If you think it _____ good, wait until you _____ it. It _____ even better! _____ Brenda's bread for **breakfast**! From the best kitchen in **Texas**.

feel   listen to   look   smells

c When you use new UltimaColor laundry detergent, your clothes _____ soft, the colors _____ bright and the fragrance _____ awesome. But don't believe us, _____ this happy customer: "I put UltimaColor in my washing **machine**, and now my clothes are super **clean**!"

hear   listen to   read   sound

d When you _____ loud rock, you don't want the music to stop. You don't have to _____ the neighbors **fight**, because your music will _____ great all **night**! Warning: loud music can cause hearing problems. _____ the safety instructions before use.

3 ▶1.2 Listen again and notice the rhymes in the **bold** words in each text.

4 ▶1.3 Listen and react personally. Follow the model.
Model: *Fresh coffee. Taste.*
You: *It tastes <u>great</u>!*
Model: *Old shoes. Smell.*
You: *They smell <u>terrible</u>.*

5 🙂 **Make it personal** Think of things you would describe with sentences a–e.
a It tastes awful.
b They smell great.
c It feels soft.
d They sound awesome.
e It looks interesting.

1.3 Do you read, hear, or watch a lot of ads?

1 ▶1.4 **Complete the dialogue with *will* or *won't*. Listen to check.**

Rachel *Iron Man*! I love it! But I can't believe Yinsen is going to die!

Chris I know, but at least Stark _____ escape, and become a super hero when he returns to America. I think they _____ make another *Iron Man* movie soon.

Rachel No, they _____, it's getting too old now. Anyway, what's for dinner?

Chris Well, I don't have much food in the kitchen. How about pizza? I _____ call and order some. I want Meat Feast. What do you want?

Rachel Hmm? I _____ have the vegetarian one, please.

2 **Order the words in a–f to make sentences.**

a will / of / she / money / take / all / probably / his / .
b die / Yinsen / will / .
c call / I / some / order / will / and / pizza / .
d get / she / married / will / .
e vegetarian one / will / I / have / the / .
f will / Stark / become / definitely / a superhero / .

3 **Mark sentences a–f in 2 as either predictions (P) or unplanned decisions (U).**

4 ▶1.5 **Listen to the rest of Chris and Rachel's dialogue. Check the two problems they have.**

a Chris doesn't get the pizza he wants.
b Chris can't afford the pizza.
c The Meat Feast smells bad.
d Rachel's pizza is too big.
e Rachel's pizza smells strange.
f Rachel doesn't want to take it home.

5 ▶1.5 **Listen again and complete a–e. Then mark them predictions (P) or unplanned decisions (U).**

a Ah, that's the pizza, _____ _____ _____.
b Oh yes that's right. _____ _____ and get it.
c Chris, it's enormous. _____ _____ _____ all that!
d I think _____ _____ _____ home with me.

6 ▶1.6 🔵 **Make it personal** **Listen and answer. Write or record your answers.**

> 🔊 **Connect**
>
> *Think of two predictions for the year 2030. Write them in a short tweet.*

7 **Complete the sentences with the words in the box.**

bubbles	countryside	cozy	leather	moist

a When it's cold I love a nice, hot bath with plenty of _____ .
b I love my new jacket. It's really _____ and warm, and it looks stylish too.
c This cake's lovely! So _____ and delicious.
d That's a nice bag. Is it real _____ ?
e We used to live in the city but then we moved to the _____ .

1.4 What shouldn't you do to stay healthy?

1 Read the introduction to the article. Underline the four suggested reasons for taking a day off.

Everybody needs a little break sometimes.

Maybe you feel stressed, maybe you have to care for your children, maybe you went out late last night or maybe it's a beautiful sunny day and you just don't want to work. Whatever your reason, here is our step-by-step guide to taking a day off work, but don't tell your boss that you read this article!

2 Read the rest of the article and match the headings to each paragraph. There is one extra heading. Then put them in the correct order, 1–4.

| Going back to work | Inform your boss | Party time! | Preparation | Your time off |

a _____

Now you are free to enjoy your time off. But be careful! If your phone rings, be careful how you answer it, it might be your boss. And if you have a lot of fun, NEVER post it on social media! In fact, it's a good idea to stay at home.

b _____

Remember to look ill when you return to the office. Watch a late-night movie so you go to work looking tired. Put a box of painkillers or cough medicine on your desk so that everyone can see it. REMEMBER! Never take medicine if you don't really need it, or you will really get sick. And your boss will get suspicious if you take more time off!

c _____

Call your boss early in the morning. Your voice will sound bad and they will be getting ready for work so they won't have time to ask any difficult questions. Keep the conversation short. Don't give too many details, but be ready to answer any questions.

d _____

Choose your illness carefully and be sure you know the right symptoms. We recommend a stomachache for a short break, and flu or a bad headache if you need more time. Try to choose something contagious so that your boss doesn't want you in the office. A few days before you plan to be "sick", start to show symptoms. A loud cough is easy to do and will get attention. You can also say that you hurt in various places, but you should try not to be too specific.

3 ▶1.7 Based on the article, give advice with **should** / **shouldn't**. Follow the model.

Model: *Investigate the symptoms.*
You: *You should investigate the symptoms.*

Model: *Give details.*
You: *You shouldn't give details.*

4 Complete the advice with **should** or **shouldn't**.

a You _____ take a day off on Mondays or Fridays. Long weekends are suspicious.
b If you can, you _____ get a letter from a doctor.
c You _____ take time off when your work is very busy—you will be unpopular with your colleagues.
d You _____ play dangerous sports. If you break your arm it will be difficult to explain!
e You _____ go to work when you have a bad cold unless the doctor tells you to.

5 ▶1.8 Read these sentences aloud and listen to check your pronunciation.
a You **shouldn't** wear **shoes** in the house.
b **Put two** painkillers in a glass of water.
c How did you **cook** this **soup**?
d This **book** is a **true** story.

6 Put the **bold** words in **5** in the correct column according to the sound of the underlined letters. Listen again to check.

/ʊ/	/uː/
shouldn't	

7 🎤 **Make it personal** What advice would you give to someone to stay healthy? Write five pieces of advice.

1.5 When do you ask for help?

1 Read five predictions about the future made in the past. Which came true?

a Gold has even now but a few years to live. The day is near when bars of it will be as common and as cheap as bars of iron or blocks of steel.
(Thomas Edison, 1911)

b We will have high-definition, wide-screen television sets and a push-button dialing system to order the movie you want at the time you want it.
(Roger Ebert, 1988)

c Nuclear-powered vacuum cleaners will probably be a reality in ten years.
(Alex Lewyt, 1955)

d There will be no C, X or Q in our everyday alphabet. They will be abandoned because unnecessary.
(John Elfreth Watkins, 1900)

e It will soon be possible to transmit wireless messages all over the world so simply that any individual can carry and operate his own apparatus.
(Nikola Tesla, 1909)

2 Complete a–e with a reflexive pronoun if necessary.
   a Can you see _____ in this photo?
   b Please wash your hands _____.
   c There's food in the kitchen, so just help _____.
   d Fredo gets up _____ at 7 a.m. every morning.
   e Then he shaves _____ and gets dressed.

3 ▶ 1.9 Listen to three dialogues and select how the person can help.

4 Divide these lines into mini dialogues.
   a Ihavetogototheairportdoyouwantmetodrivethat'svery kindofyou.
   b I'mgoingtowashthedisheswouldyoulikemetodryyesplease.
   c Thesebagsarereallyheavyl'llcarryoneforyouthat'sverykindofyou.
   d Idon'tunderstandthisproblemdoyouwantahandyesplease.
   e It'sreallycoldinheredoyouwantmetoturnofftheac thanksfortheofferbutIcandoit.

   I have to go to the airport.
   Do you want me to drive?
   That's very kind of you.

5 Put the words in the correct order to make offers.
   a hand / you / a / need / Do ?
   b to / me / Would / help / like / you ?
   c me / Do / you / want / off / music / the / turn / to ?
   d you / I / Can / help ?

> **Can you remember ...**
> ▶ 10 life priorities? SB→p.6
> ▶ the 5 senses and verbs to talk about them? SB→p.8
> ▶ how to make ⊕ and ⊖ predictions? SB→p.10
> ▶ 7 common illnesses? SB→p.12
> ▶ how to make ⊕⊖ sentences with *should*? SB→p.12
> ▶ ways to offer help and how to accept and refuse help? SB→p.15

2.1 Do you ever read newspapers?

1 Read the article, then label a–e in the graph with:

~~Generally~~   Internet   Newspapers   Today   TV

● Newspapers Are Dead! Long Live the Internet!

Newspaper circulation is declining, and now more people get their news on the Internet than ever before. In a recent survey we asked commuters on the morning train two questions: "Where do you generally get your news?" and "If you saw the news today, what format was it in?".

Our results show that generally the Internet is now more popular than newspapers for news, although TV is still the most popular. Interestingly, when we asked where people got their news today, more people said newspapers than the Internet. Maybe this is because people read the news on the Internet on their lunch break at work, but read newspapers in the morning.

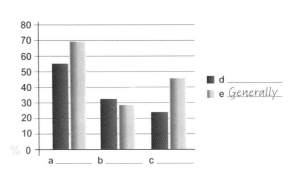

d _____
e _Generally_

a ____ b ____ c ____

2 According to the article and graph, are a–c True (T) or False (F)?
 a More people got today's news from a newspaper than online.
 b More than half usually get their news from the Internet.
 c The time of day affected the survey.

3 ▶2.1 Match the phrases with the correct preposition. Listen to a monologue to check.

an article   a magazine   the front page   the sports section   a tablet   TV

in	on

4 ▶2.1 Listen again and complete a–f with two words.
 a He only gets a newspaper o_____ S_____s.
 b He thinks the editorial articles are v_____ i_____.
 c On weekends, he reads the s_____ s_____.
 d The TV guide is in _____ m_____.
 e He thinks the rest of the magazine is a w_____ of p_____.
 f From Monday to Friday he reads important items on t_____ l_____.

🔊 Connect

Find an interesting news article online, then summarize it to a classmate.

5 Circle the correct options in sentences a–f.
 a **Yesterday / Yesterday's** news **was / were** very sad.
 b I only **look at / see** the photos **in / on** newspapers.
 c It's easy to **lose / waste** time **in / on** the Internet.
 d My brother has a lot of books **in / on** his shelves.
 e I sometimes read a novel **in / on** the bath.
 f We have a lot **of / in** common.

6 ▶2.2 **Make it personal** Listen to questions a–e and check your answers.
 a ☐ Every day.   ☐ Once a week.   ☐ Only sometimes.   ☐ Other.
 b ☐ I'm always connected. ☐ Once a day.   ☐ No, never.   ☐ Never.
 c ☐ Yes, always.   ☐ Yes, sometimes.   ☐ Yes, but it depends on
 d ☐ Yes, I love it. ☐ No, I think it's stupid. the celebrity.
 e ☐ Yes, I did.   ☐ No, I didn't.

9

2.2 What were you doing at 8 o'clock last night?

1 Choose the correct verb form.
   a What **were you liking** / **did you like** watching when you were a child?
   b I **watched** / **was watching** TV at 8 p.m. last night.
   c We both **loved** / **were loving** that movie.
   d I **was talking** / **talked** to Anna when you called.
   e Misha **played** / **was playing** video games at 10 p.m. last night.

2 ▶2.3 *Excuses, Excuses!* Order the words to make questions and complete the replies. Listen to check.
   a **Mother:** you / fighting / why / were / ?
      Sons: We _____ (not fight). We _____ (play).
   b **Boss:** Why were you on the Internet? weren't / why / working / you / ?
      Employee: I _____ (send) an e-mail to a client.
   c **Angry girlfriend:** Is this SMS from your ex-girlfriend? was / you / why / texting / she / ?
      Boyfriend: She _____ (ask) for a friend's phone number.
   d **Angry boyfriend:** you / me / didn't / call / why / ?
      Girlfriend: Sorry, but my phone _____ (not work).

3 ▶2.3 These words from **2** have silent letters. Practice saying them, then listen again to check.

   > fight   phone   friend   why

4 ▶2.4 Listen and respond with a reason from **3** after the beep.

5 *State or Action?* Complete a–f with the verbs in the simple past or past continuous.

a I _____ (not eat) it, I _____ (taste) a little.

b _____ the milk _____ (taste) OK this morning?

c _____ you _____ (have) a headache yesterday?

d Sorry, I _____ (have) breakfast when you called.

e _____ you _____ (like) the video I sent to you?

f I'm sorry, I _____ (not listen). What did you say?

6 **Make it personal** What were you doing at these times yesterday? Record your answers.

   > 7 a.m.   11:30 a.m.   1:15 p.m.   4 p.m.   6:30 p.m.   8 p.m.

Connect

Choose a photo on your phone. Write a short description of what you were doing when you took it.

2.3 What's the world's most serious problem?

1 ▶2.5 **Listen to extracts a–h and match them with the problems below.**

- ☐ animal extinction
- ☐ climate change
- ☐ corruption
- ☐ crime
- ☐ disease
- ☐ pollution
- ☐ poverty
- ☐ unemployment

2 ▶2.5 **Listen again and match the numbers below to extracts a–h. There's one extra number.**

- ☐ 1
- ☐ 13
- ☐ 30
- ☐ 88.2%
- ☐ 2,300
- ☐ 3,200
- ☐ 200,000
- ☐ 2,800,000
- ☐ 200,000,000

3 Match the words to definitions a–i.

a A large curve of different colors which can appear in the sky when there's sun and rain.

b When the moon goes between the Earth and the sun.

c A sudden shaking of the Earth's surface.

d A fire that moves quickly and out of control.

e A huge storm that moves over water.

f A long period of no rain when there isn't enough water for plants and animals to live.

g A very large wave, usually caused by an earthquake at sea.

h When a place becomes covered with water.

i A storm with thunder and lightning.

- ☐ a hurricane
- ☐ a rainbow
- ☐ a flood
- ☐ a thunderstorm
- ☐ an eclipse
- ☐ a tsunami
- ☐ an earthquake
- ☐ a wildfire
- ☐ a drought

🔊 Connect

Search online about one of the types of natural phenomena in 3. Read about it, then share what you found out with a classmate.

4 Complete the posts with the words in the box and the past continuous of the verbs in parentheses.

> drought   earthquakes   eclipse   flood
> hurricane   lightning   rainbow   thunderstorm

Weird Weather Website

a Yesterday, there was an _____. It was really strange. When the sun went behind the moon, the temperature dropped for a few minutes. We _____ (watch) it in our yard with a special protective mask. It was amazing. BTW, I read a theory that this causes _____. Did anybody feel the ground move?

b During the first few months of this year there was a _____. There was no water, so the plants _____ (not grow). I work in agriculture, so I really depend on the weather. I won't make much money this year.

c There was a _____ in my town last night. There's a lot of water damage to buildings and possessions. Thankfully, I _____ (stay) with my grandparents, so I didn't have to move, but my neighbors had to leave their houses in the middle of the night.

d I love photography and I _____ (play) with my new camera the other afternoon when suddenly the sky went dark. There were these huge black clouds and a few hours later, a _____ started. I took some photos of the _____ hitting the ground. They're great photos, I'll post some.

e I _____ (watch) TV last night. It was a program about _____ Katrina in New Orleans. It was terrible. We don't get weather like that here, in fact, it _____ (rain) a few moments ago and now the sun is out and there's a beautiful _____.

5 ▶2.6 **Read the three poems and underline the picture word sounds in each one. Listen to check.**

a *I have two young cousins.*
I call them "double trouble."
Everywhere they go they cause
problems for their mother.   /ʌ/

b *This is a story about a house in the clouds,*
Two thousand steps up, three thousand steps down.
The sun was hot in summer,
The wind was loud at night.
The couple couldn't live there,
So they found a place in town.   /aʊ/

c *It would be good to visit Hollywood.*
If you get a chance to go, you should.   /ʊ/

6 ▶2.7 🅐 **Make it personal** **Listen and answer. Write or record your answers.**

11

2.4 Was your mom living here when you were born?

1 ▶2.8 Listen to stories 1–3 and match two of photos a–f to each of them.

2 Use the photos to complete sentences a–c with the simple past or past continuous of the verbs in parentheses.

a Abby _____ (work) with some kids when suddenly the door _____ (open) and Meghan and Harry _____ (walk) in!
b Pete _____ (watch) TV when he _____ (hear) a loud BANG.
c Zoe _____ (talk) to some people on the bus and they _____ (offer) her a job.

3 Choose the correct alternatives.

a When I was a child I **didn't like / wasn't liking** broccoli.
b What **were you doing / did you do** when I **phoned / I was phoning** you last night?
c Paulo **was chatting / chatted** online when the power **went out / was going out**.
d What **were you talking / did you talk** about when I **came / was coming** in?
e Chiara **was walking / walked** downstairs when her heel **was breaking / broke**.

4 Correct two mistakes in each sentence.

a When I was more young I was playing a lot of video games.
b My phone was ringing when I was in middle of taking a test at school.
c My friends wasn't smiling when I was taking a photo of them.
d What you were doing the last night when the outage happened?

5 ▶2.9 Listen to sound effect stories a–d. Use the words to tell each one in a single sentence.

a walk / street / start / rain
b work / be / power outage
c jog / park / dog / attack
d play / piano / cat / jump

6 🅜 **Make it personal** Mark which events a–e you have experienced, and write a sentence about each.

What were you doing the last time there was…

a a power outage? ( )
The last time there was a power outage, I was watching TV at home.

b a thunderstorm? ( )
_____
_____
_____

c an earthquake? ( )
_____
_____
_____

d a flood? ( )
_____
_____
_____

e an eclipse? ( )
_____
_____
_____

2.5 What do you carry in your pockets?

1 ▶ 2.10 **Order the pieces of paper, 1–12, to make a joke. Can you guess the ending? Listen to check.**

[1] A man and his wife were having some…	☐ … message: *Please wake me up at 4:30 a.m.* He put the message on the TV and…
☐ … he woke up and looked at his alarm clock. It was 10:30 a.m.!	[2] … problems in their marriage and they weren't…
☐ … to watch her favorite drama show every evening. One day, the man came…	☐ … talking to each other. Their house was completely…
☐ … the next morning. But he didn't want to talk to his wife, so he wrote a…	☐ A piece of paper was lying on the table next to his alarm clock. It said:
☐ … he went to bed. In the morning…	☐ … home from work. He was tired and he had to catch a plane early…
☐ _____	☐ … silent. Only the TV made noise at night because the woman liked…

2 ▶ 2.11 **Listen to some more anecdotes and respond with one of these phrases after the beep.**

> No! You're joking!

> Oh dear. That's bad luck.

> Wow! That is lucky.

3 ▶ 2.12 **Listen to a firefighter from the story "Strange Things Happen". At each beep, choose the best question.**

a ☐ What happened?
  ☐ Where did you go?
b ☐ Where was the house?
  ☐ Why was she on fire?

c ☐ They were in her pocket?
  ☐ The stones caught fire?
d ☐ Is she OK?
  ☐ Can you buy these stones?

4 ▶ 2.13 **🅐 Make it personal** **Listen and match answers a–e to the questions.**

☐ Did you read the news today?
☐ Is crime a big problem in your area?
☐ What kind of TV shows do you like?
☐ Do you remember the 2011 tsunami?
☐ Do you know any funny stories?

a No, it's very safe where I live.
b Nah, I can never remember jokes. But my brother knows a lot.
c Yeah, the front page had a story about politics.
d Yeah, I saw it on the news. It was terrible.
e Hmm. I like comedies and dramas.

🔊 Connect

Write your own answers to the questions in 4 and send them to a friend or your teacher.

Can you remember …

➤ 7 news genres? SB→p.19
➤ Past *be + -ing* ⊕ ⊖ ❓? SB→p.20
➤ 8 global problems? SB→p.22
➤ 9 natural phenomena? SB→p.23
➤ 2 words to connect past continuous and simple past clauses? SB→p.24
➤ 3 ways to show you're listening? SB→p.27
➤ 8 phrases to react to positive or negative things? SB→p.27

13

3.1 How often do you travel?

1 Match the verbs and nouns. Then number them in a logical order.

pack	in line ___
board	your bags ___
be stopped at	a ticket _1_
book	the plane ___
take	customs ___
have	a taxi to the airport ___
stand	to your hotel ___
check in	a snack on the plane ___

2 Read three travel stories, then complete 1–8 with the correct form of these verbs.

arrive   board   book   break down
crowded   hitchhike   miss   pack

3 ▶ 3.1 Circle the correct words in bold in the stories. Then listen to check.

4 Reread and answer a–e.
 a Which person didn't like the other passengers?
 b Which two people were scared?
 c Who didn't want to hitchhike?
 d Who is the youngest traveler?
 e Which person was traveling alone?

5 🎧 **Make it personal** Order the words in a–d to make questions. Circle the best answer for you.
 a go / do / stressed / get / when / you / wrong / things / ?

 _____
 Never. / Sometimes. / Often.

 b well / last / did / go / your / vacation / ?

 _____
 It was a disaster. / It was OK. / I had a great time.

 c get / when / bus / you / you / miss / do / angry / the / ?

 _____
 No, I wait for the next one. / Only if I'm going to an important place. / Always. I hate being late.

 d impatient / you / kids / on / get / young / do / planes / with / ?

 _____
 No, I love kids. / Only if they are loud. / Yes, kids shouldn't be permitted on planes.

Person 1 Last weekend I went **in / on** the worst trip ever. It was Saturday and Mom decided that we were all going to the beach for the day. So we _____ ¹ our bags with bathing suits and started **in / on** the two-hour drive. Dad was driving but he doesn't like the GPS. This was fine **in / on** the highway but, after about 30 minutes **in / on** the back roads, Dad started to look worried. We were lost! Mom got the map and soon they were both arguing about which road to take and which direction to go in. And **in / on** the back of the car things weren't much better. My brother can sleep anywhere at any time, too, and that was exactly what he was doing. His head was falling **in / on** my arm, and when I pushed him away, he woke up and started crying. This continued until we finally _____ ² at the beach, four hours after we left home. And guess what? It was raining, and I _____ ³ my friend's party, too! Never again!

Person 2 Around four years ago I was traveling **in / on** India. I took a lot of night buses and they were usually great. _____ ⁴ your ticket, find your seat, fall asleep. It was easy. And this time everything was going well until… SMASH! One of the windows fell from the bus. Suddenly a cold wind was blowing around us, and I mean cold! The driver continued, and I put **in / on** my sweater and shared a blanket with another passenger until… BANG! And the bus slowly stopped. This time it was the engine and the driver couldn't continue. The bus _____ ⁵ **in / on** the middle of the night, **in / on** the middle of the road, **in / on** the middle of nowhere. We were stuck and just had to wait. Some passengers _____ ⁶ in passing trucks, but I was too scared. I can laugh about it now, but at the time it was terrible.

Person 3 OMG, what **a / –** day! I usually drive, but today I took **a / the** train for **a / the** first time on a Saturday—never again! Those soccer fans are crazy! I was going home with Bruna, and **a / the** train was nice and quiet, and then we got to **the / –** stadium. The station was _____ ⁷ with thousands of fans, and they all looked violent and scary and **the / –** police had bulletproof vests and **the / –** dogs and everything. **The / –** fans _____ ⁸ the train, and they were shouting and using **a / –** bad language—it was terrible. But then **– / the** worst thing was they started jumping up and down. I couldn't believe it. **The / A** train actually started moving from side to side. It was **a / –** really dangerous. I was terrified!

3.2 Have you ever been to another country?

1 ▶ 3.2 Listen and complete the survey for Tanya.

The Internet has changed many aspects of modern life: the way we communicate, get information, work, etc. Even the way we think and act has changed. And shopping has changed dramatically too. Have you bought any of these things online? Please check ✓ the boxes on the computer screen.

	This month	In the last 6 months	Never
books	✓		
music			
movies			
travel tickets			
hotel rooms			
event tickets			
electronic equipment			
clothes			

2 Use the survey in **1** to write present perfect sentences and questions.

a Tanya / buy / books / this month / .
   Tanya has bought books online this month.

b what / you / buy / online / this month / ?

c she / watch / a movie online / twice this month / .

d you / ever / book / a hotel online / ?

e she / book / travel tickets online / .

f she / go shopping / today / .

3 🎧 **Make it personal** Complete the survey with your own answers and sentences.
I've never bought a book online!

4 Use these ideas to make guesses about your class.

eat crocodile	try martial arts
go abroad	give money to charity
see a celebrity	plant a tree

a I think no one in my class has …
b At least three people have …
c Only one person …
d I think my best friend …
e I think my teacher …

5 Order the words in a–i to make questions. Which experiences in **4** do they refer to?

a lake / where / the / was / ?
b you / it / when / wear / did / ?
c often / money / how / give / you / do / ?
d him or her / did / speak / you / to / ?
e did / like / what / taste / it / ?
f you / did / it / where / plant / ?
g you / vacation / go / did / on / ?
h you / me / something / can / teach / ?
i did / long / for / how / you / fly / ?

6 Correct two mistakes in each of a–d.

a Have you ever swimmed in a lake? No, but I have swum in a river when I was on vacation.
b The last time I have worn a tie was when I was at the school.
c You have ever buy clothes online?
d Have you gone abroad ever? Yes, I have been in Canada twice.

7 ▶ 3.3 Match the words to the sound pictures. Listen to check. Notice the different spellings.

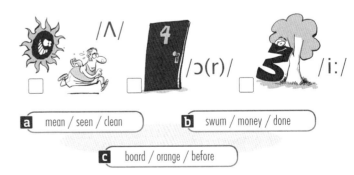

a mean / seen / clean
b swum / money / done
c board / orange / before

8 🎧 **Make it personal** Which of the sentences in **6** are true for you? Record your answers.

3.3 Have you sung a song in English yet?

1 ▶ 3.4 A couple are preparing to go on vacation. Listen and order the photos, 1–4, as they mention them.

2 ▶ 3.4 Add *just*, *yet* or *already* to extracts a–e. Listen again to check.
   a The dogsitter hasn't arrived.
   b I've told you.
   c Have you fed the dog?
   d I've bought some food for her.
   e I've remembered!

3 Circle the correct meanings for extracts a–e.
   a He's late again. – *'s* means **is** / **has**.
   b Just a minute. – *just* means **recently** / **only**.
   c I've just finished eating. – *just* means **recently** / **only**.
   d I've already bought some food. – *already* means **all prepared** / **before now**.
   e OK. All ready? Let's go. – *all ready* means **all prepared** / **before now**.

4 **Make it personal** What has happened today? Write sentences with *just*, *already* and *yet*.
   a I / have breakfast
   I've already had breakfast. / I haven't had breakfast yet. / I've just had breakfast.
   b I / go online
   c My friend / call me
   d I / leave home
   e I / eat dinner
   f I / take a shower
   g I / check my email
   h I / do a lot of exercise

5 **Web Hunt!** Read the article. Then go online to research the four projects. Mark them **A**, **B** or **C**.
   A: Construction has not started yet.
   B: Construction has already started.
   C: Construction has finished.

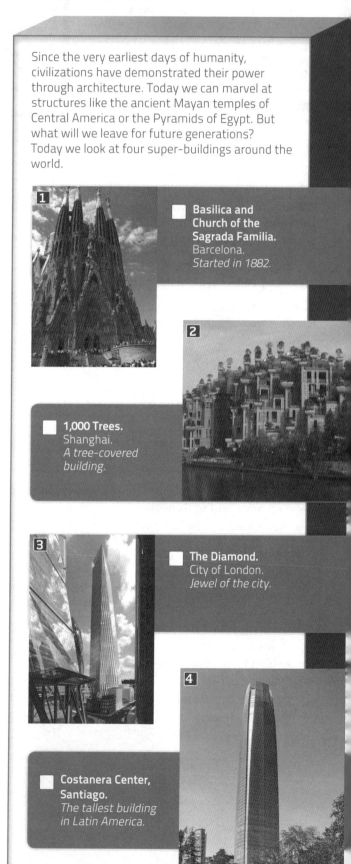

Since the very earliest days of humanity, civilizations have demonstrated their power through architecture. Today we can marvel at structures like the ancient Mayan temples of Central America or the Pyramids of Egypt. But what will we leave for future generations? Today we look at four super-buildings around the world.

1 Basilica and Church of the Sagrada Familia. Barcelona. *Started in 1882.*

2 1,000 Trees. Shanghai. *A tree-covered building.*

3 The Diamond. City of London. *Jewel of the city.*

4 Costanera Center, Santiago. *The tallest building in Latin America.*

16

3.4 How long have you lived here?

1 Match choices a–e to the reasons.

a   I'm volunteering in a school

b   I decided to travel for a year

c   I didn't take a gap year, I went straight to college

d   I spent two years working before college

e   I decided to try lots of different jobs

☐ as I don't want to waste my time traveling or volunteering.

☐ because I didn't really know what I wanted to do and college is sometimes a waste of time.

☐ to earn money. Studying is expensive!

☐ because I want to be a teacher after college and the experience will help me get a job.

☐ to learn about different cultures and see the world.

2 Read an interview from a student magazine. Which choice from **1**, a–e, best describes him?

Marvin Powers—Self-Made Millionaire

a You are very successful. Tell us, what do you do?
Right now, I am the director of a transportation company. When I started it, we only had three trucks… ☐

b Very impressive. How long have you had the business?
Not very long… ☐

c That is a short time! Did you study logistics at college?
No, I didn't go to college… ☐

d So where did you learn to be a businessman?
I guess I studied at the University of Life!… ☐

e OK. So what has been the most important lesson you've learned?
Ummm. I guess the most important thing is to learn from your mistakes… ☐

f Good advice. Now, apart from your business successes, what are you most proud of in your life?
It has to be my family: my two daughters and my beautiful wife… ☐

g Congratulations. And now our final question. What do you do to relax?
Ummm. I don't really have time to relax. I played soccer and went to the movies a lot when I was younger… ☐

3 Complete with *for* or *since*. Then use these sentences to complete a–g in **2**.

a   … I've done a lot of jobs *since* I left school.

b   … I think that studying _____ three or four years is a waste of time.

c   … We've been married _____ almost eight years now.

d   … And I've made a lot of them _____ I started out in the big, bad world!

e   … I guess I've been in this business _____ about six years.

f   … But I haven't done that _____ a long time.

g   … _____ then, it has grown to over fifty vehicles.

4 ▶3.5 Follow the model. Listen and answer with *for* and *since*.

Model: *How long / live in your house?*
You: *How long have you lived in your house?*
Model: *October.*
You: *Since October.*

Model: *How long / live in this city?*
You: *How long have you lived in this city?*
Model: *Five years.*
You: *For five years.*

5 ▶3.5 🔵 **Make it personal**   Listen again but now give your own answers.

🔊 Connect

Interview your partner using the questions and record it on your phone.

17

3.5 Are you a logical person?

1 Read and complete the introduction to an article with the correct form of **have** or **be**.

MONSTER MYTH

Humans _____ always _____ a fascination for strange creatures. From the Himalayan yeti to the Chinese dragon, every culture _____ a terrifying monster or mysterious giant to populate their stories, to make children _____ good and, nowadays, to attract tourists. Here _____ one of our favorites.

2 Complete 1–11 in the text with these suffixes.

-ic   -ment   -al   -ion

☐ They have even taken photographs to support their convict___s¹, but they are never clear, and so there is no corroborat___² for the story.

[1] Nessie, or the Loch Ness Monster, lives in a deep lake in Scotland and swims to other lakes through underground tunnels. The perfect environ___³ for a monster!

☐ Many people believe that Nessie is not a monster and is, in fact, a dinosaur that has survived since pre-histor___⁴ times in the lake.

☐ In 2003, a team did a scientif___⁵ investigat___⁶ of the lake. They used sonar equip___⁷ and satellite technology capable of extreme precis___⁸ and they found…

☐ However, despite this long existence, the monster myth only started in 1933. And so the argu___⁹ between Nessie believers and non-believers was born.

☐ Believers have come to this remote locat___¹⁰ for almost a century hoping to see the famous monster, and there have been occasion___¹¹ reports of the reptile.

☐ You guessed it. Absolutely nothing.

3 ▶3.6 Reread and order the rest of the article, 1–7. Listen to check.

4 ▶3.7 Listen to four dialogues and complete the reactions 1–4.

5 ▶3.7 Listen again and repeat the reaction after the beep.

Connect
Tell your partner about something surprising. Record their reaction on your phone.

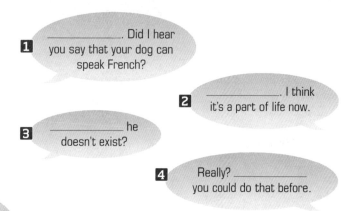

1 _____. Did I hear you say that your dog can speak French?

2 _____. I think it's a part of life now.

3 _____ he doesn't exist?

4 Really? _____ you could do that before.

Can you remember …
- 7 stages of a trip? SB→p. 32
- 4 past participle verbs? SB→p. 34
- how to ask about past experiences and how to ask follow-up questions? SB→p. 34
- which adverb means a past experience was very recent? SB→p. 37
- 2 words to use when you talk about the duration of an action? SB→p. 39
- 4 suffix endings to make nouns or adjectives? SB→p. 41

4.1 Were you spoiled as a child?

1 What's the form of the underlined verbs in questions a–b: infinitive or past?
   a How old were you when you <u>went</u> to your first school?
   b When did you <u>go</u> to your first school?

2 Complete a–f with the correct form of the verbs.
   a How old were you when you _____ (buy) your first pair of shoes on your own?
   b How old were you when you _____ (get) your first cell phone?
   c Do you remember when you _____ (take) your first exam?
   d When did you _____ (go) on your first date?
   e How old were you when you _____ (go) to your first party without your parents?
   f When was the last time you _____ (laugh) a lot?

Connect
Interview your partner with the questions and record it on your phone.

3 Read the first part of the article. True (T) or False (F)?
   a Only Japanese people believe that blood type affects personality.
   b People use blood type to predict more than just personality.
   c Many scientists accept the connection between blood type and personality.

It's in the blood

Do you believe that the stars really determine our personalities? Why not something a little closer to home, a little more… biological? Well, in Japan and South Korea that is exactly what they believe. Over there, your blood type predicts your personality… and a whole lot more too. It all sounds very scientific, right? Wrong, there is very little scientific evidence.

4 Read the rest of the article and match adjectives 1–16 to each blood type.

1 active   7 hardworking   13 sensitive
2 aggressive   8 honest   14 shy
3 creative   9 independent   15 sociable
4 critical   10 responsible   16 spoiled
5 curious   11 kind
6 funny   12 obedient

Type A
These people like to help other people and they are good listeners. However, they don't like to share their emotions and sometimes cry when other people are critical of them. This means they sometimes spend time alone, but they don't mind that. They can also be very obsessive about small details.
Career: s_ftw_r_ _ng_n__r,   l_br_r__n.

Type B
These are the artists and the explorers. They love making new things, experimenting and discovering how things work. And they don't like taking orders—they want to do things their way. This means that they often ignore their duties and obligations.
Career: c__k,   h__r styl_st,   j__rn_l_st.

Type AB
These people want to succeed, and they will really work for it. If their boss or teacher asks them to do something, they will do it without any questions. They hate to see bad work or lazy workers and they will share their opinions and their feelings. Sometimes this is good, but not always!
Career: l_wy_r,   t__cher.

Type O
These people love to be the center of attention. They love to make new friends and they are always joking and always doing something exciting. However, if they don't get what they want they can quickly change, and sometimes they try to get what they want physically.
Career: _thl_te,   b_nk m_n_g_r,   p_l_t_c__n.

5 ▶4.1 Complete the career words with vowels. Listen to check.

6 **Make it personal** Answer questions a–f in 2 about yourself.

4.2 What did you use to do as a child?

1 ▶4.2 Order pictures a–g to make a story. Listen to check.

2 ▶4.3 Listen and complete an interview for ID with Silvio Roma, an Italian immigrant.

ID So, Silvio. _____ use to work a lot at school?
Silvio No, I didn't. But I used to _____.
ID Uh-huh. And _____ did you use to play?
Silvio I used to play soccer every day _____ young.
ID What _____ before you came here?
Silvio I lived in Milan and I _____ to college. I was a music student.
ID And do you like this country?
Silvio Well, I _____ like it. It was very strange coming to a new country with a different language. But now I am very happy here.

3 ▶4.4 You are Silvio! Use the answers in **2** and make sentences with *used to*. Follow the model.
Model: *not / like school*
You: *I didn't use to like school.*
Model: *love playing sports*
You: *I used to love playing sports.*

4 Match the two parts of sentences a–d.
a My parents didn't use to let me watch TV after 9 p.m.
b I used to have a lot of CDs
c I used to play sports a lot more
d I didn't use to like English

☐ but I think it's OK now.
☐ than I do now.
☐ when I was young.
☐ before I bought an MP3 player.

5 🎧 **Make it personal** Order the words in a–c to make questions. Then answer them.
a you / used / school / who / take / to / to / ?
b did / to / cartoons / use / watch / which / you / ?
c food / hate / what / use / to / did / you / ?

📶 **Connect**
Record your answers on your phone. Send them to a classmate or your teacher.

6 ▶4.5 Listen and cross out four silent *t*s in these words.

advantage   castle   Christmas   digital   kitchen   listen   often   turntable   watch

4.3 Has your taste in music changed?

1 Use the clues to complete the crossword.

ACROSS
1 round, black things which play music
5 popular music
6 playing music over the Internet
7 what records are made from

DOWN
2 transfer something from the Internet to your computer or mobile device
3 digital music files
4 a machine which plays vinyl records
5 an old type of music from the 70s

2 Read quotes 1–5 about music. Which talk about the past (PA)? Which talk about the present (PR)? Which talk about both (B)?

1 "I don't really like pop music at all. It all sounds the same to me. I like rock music much more. I actually play guitar in a rock band, and we write all our own music."

2 "My parents used to listen to punk music when they were teenagers. They used to wear really weird clothes and go to concerts and just jump around for hours. I saw a photo of them and it was really embarrassing, they were wearing very strange clothes!"

3 "When I was a teenager I used to listen to heavy metal music. I had long hair and only wore black clothes. I thought I was very cool, but nowadays I just think I was a bit silly."

4 "I love electronic music, and I make my own music alone on my computer. I don't do it to become famous or anything, it's just a hobby and something I do in my free time. If you're interested, you can listen to my music online."

5 "I used to have a huge CD collection. I think I had over 500! Then one day I decided to sell them and buy all the music as MP3s. I miss my collection now though, I still have all the music on MP3s, but it's not the same as having a big collection you can look through and organize."

3 Read the quotes again and write the number of the person who …
a thinks their parents were weird.
b thinks a type of music sounds the same.
c regrets something they did with their music collection.
d thinks differently now to how they did when they were a teenager.
e makes music on their own.
f plays a musical instrument.
g talks about the clothes they used to wear.

4 **Make it personal** Answer a–d.
a What music did you use to listen to when you were younger?
b Do you still like this music now? Why (not)?
c What's your favorite way to listen to music?
d What music DON'T you like? Why not?

Connect
Record your answers and email them to a friend or your teacher, or write them as a tweet.

4.4 Do you speak English as often as possible?

1 Read the reviews and match the highlighted adjectives to their opposites.

big   easy   expensive   heavy   unclear   unpopular

TECH REVIEW

Star 100
The *Star* is a very popular piece of equipment. It is the biggest and heaviest of the tablets here. One disadvantage of the *Star* is usability. Many people find it difficult to use.

Price: $299
Dimensions: 24 × 18 cm. 660 g
Screen: 146 pixels per cm
Memory: 512GB
Usability: ★★★☆☆

Eye-let Mini
The *Eye-let Mini* is selling very quickly. Most people love its user interface (UI) and we agree. It is very, very easy to use. It is also relatively small and light so it is easy to carry. However, it has quite a small memory, only 128GB.

Price: $299
Dimensions: 20 × 13 cm. 312 g
Screen: 128 pixels per cm
Memory: 128GB
Usability: ★★★★★

Dall P45
The *Dall P45* will be in stores soon. The big advantage of the *P45* is the picture; with 204 ppcm it is really clear. We watched some movies online and they were perfect! And at $250, it is quite cheap.

Price: $250
Dimensions: 22 × 15 cm. 314 g
Screen: 204 pixels per cm
Memory: 512GB
Usability: ★★★★☆

2 Mark all ten adjectives Type A, Type B or Type C using the chart on Student's Book p. 50.

3 Use the information in the reviews to make sentences about the tablets.
   a The Star's picture / clear. *The Star's picture is the clearest.*
   b The Eye-let Mini / expensive / the Star. *The Eye-let Mini is as expensive as the Star.*
   c The Dall P45's memory / big / the Star's. _____
   d The Dall P45's picture / clear / the Eye-let Mini's. _____
   e The Dall P45 / not / easy to use / the Eye-let Mini. _____
   f The Eye-let Mini / about / big / the Dall P45. _____
   g The Dall P45 / cheap. _____

4 ▶ 4.6 Read sentences from **3**, one at a time after each beep. Listen to check your pronunciation and then read it again. Follow the model.
Model: *The Star's picture is the clearest.*
You: *The Star's picture is the clearest.*

5 **Make it personal** Which tablet would you choose? Complete the sentence below with all the reasons you can think of.
   I would choose the _____ because it _____ .

Connect
Send your answers to **5** to a classmate. Compare. Who has the most and best reasons?

4.5 How many pets have you had?

1 Order this story, 1–4, about an intelligent dog.

AMAZING PETS

Each lesson is five hours but Chaser loves learning, so if her owner doesn't want to teach, Chaser makes him! She is a very enthusiastic student! ☐

Have you ever tried to learn a foreign language? If you have, then you know how difficult it is to remember new words. [1]

How did it start? Well, Chaser's owner read about a dog in Germany that knew about 200 words so he decided to give his dog some lessons. ☐

Well, maybe you should take some advice from Chaser the dog. Chaser learns one or two new words every day and already has a vocabulary list of over 1,000 nouns. And now she is learning verbs too! ☐

2 Match the sentences and join them with *so* or *but*.

a I walk my dog at the same time every day
b I have a dog and two cats
c My dog doesn't like dog biscuits
d I love dogs
e Our dog has a lot of energy
f I don't have time for a dog

☐ I live in an apartment so I can't have one.
☐ we play with her a lot.
☐ I bought a goldfish.
☐ they never fight.
☐ she knows what time to go.
☐ she loves cake.

3 ▶4.7 Listen to a woman shopping and check the right answers.

a She is buying a gift for
☐ her husband. ☐ her son. ☐ her nephew.
b He is going to be
☐ 20. ☐ 21. ☐ 22.
c She wants to spend around
☐ $12. ☐ $20. ☐ $200.
d She decides to give him
☐ money. ☐ a book. ☐ a tablet.

4 ▶4.8 Match a–d to the correct endings to make suggestions. Listen to check and repeat.

a That is an important birthday. You should definitely
b Have you considered
c Twenty dollars? Have you thought about
d 21-year-olds always need money. Why don't you
☐ buying him some new technology?
☐ just give him some money so he can buy what he wants.
☐ get him something special.
☐ getting him a nice book?

5 ▶4.9 Listen and match answers a–e to these questions. Listen again and give your own answers.

☐ What blood type are you?
☐ Do you always do your homework?
☐ Did you use to hate any food?
☐ Do you like buying technology?
☐ Is 21 a special birthday in your country?

a Yeah, I love having the latest technology, but it is very expensive!
b I didn't use to like tomatoes, but I can eat them now.
c Uh, I don't know. I know O is the most common, so maybe I have type O blood.
d Uh, I think 18 is more special, and the 16th birthday is more important for girls.
e I usually do, although I'm sometimes busy doing other things.

🔊 **Connect**

Record your answers on your phone. Send them to a classmate or your teacher.

6 Choose the correct alternatives.

a Why don't you **have** / **having** a rest? You look tired.
b You should definitely **talk** / **talking** to Kate about it.
c Have you thought about **buy** / **buying** a new car?
d Have you considered **ask** / **asking** Janice for help?

Can you remember ...

➤ 16 personality adjectives? SB→p.44
➤ 11 *make* and *do* phrases? SB→p.45
➤ *used to* in ⊕, ⊖ and ❓ forms? SB→p.47
➤ 2 forms of comparatives and superlatives adjectives? SB→p.50
➤ 1 word to link a consequence? SB→p.52
➤ 1 word to make a contrast? SB→p.52
➤ 4 ways to make recommendations? SB→p.53

5

5.1 What would you like to study?

1 Cross out the school subjects in the word snake to find the hidden statement. How strongly do you agree with it?

  1 completely agree   2 partly agree   3 don't agree

youartgetbiologyasmucomputersystemscheeconomicsducageographytioliteraturenoumathematicstsidephysicsschpoliticsoolpsychologyassociologyin

2 Complete the stressed syllables in the following subjects.

☐ __ __ __ __ iness   ☐ __ __ __ __ mistry   ☐ engi __ __ __ __ ring

☐ __ __ __ __ guages   ☐ l __ __ __

3 🔵 **Make it personal** Check the subjects in **1** and **2** that you study / used to study in school. Double check the ones you get / got good grades in. Email your answers to a friend to compare.

4 ▶5.1 Listen and match people 1–5 to their degree subjects in **2**.

5 Circle the correct option in a–d.

  a He has a master's **of** / **in** history.   c They study **at** / **in** the State University.

  b She studies **at** / **in** New York.   d She studies **—** / **in** math.

6 ▶5.2 Listen to Helen and Janet, then match them to the information in the chart.

College		Marlbury ☐	Arleston ☐	Brinton ☐
Why did you choose this college?		it has a great reputation	I can get here easily ☐	it's a long way from home ☐
What do you like about the college?		an attractive campus ☐	modern facilities ☐	babysitting facilities ☐
Degree	a Helen b Janet	master's in chemistry ☐	vocational certificate in cooking ☐	bachelor's in business ☐
Why do you like this subject?		the evening classes ☐	the good teachers ☐	the excellent technology ☐
Ambition		make a million dollars a month ☐	open a café ☐	develop new medicines ☐

7 ▶5.2 Listen again and use their answers as a model to write four sentences about Leona.

Hi, I'm...

8 🔵 **Make it personal** Now write four sentences about you, your school and your plans. Use the model in **7**.

📶 **Connect**

Record your sentences on your phone. Send them to a classmate or your teacher.

24

5.2 What do you have to do tonight?

1 Read Carrie's school journal and match two of these activities to each day.

a an exam
b an exercise
c a group work activity
d homework
e a pair work activity
f a paper
g a project
h a quiz
i a summary
j a journal entry

Monday 21st _foreign languages_

[b] First we did an activity—matching vocabulary to
[c] pictures and practicing the pronunciation. That was good because my pronunciation is terrible and I learned some new words. Then we had to discuss the effects of pollution on our city. I worked with Sandra, Rafael and Nathalia. It was kind of interesting, but Rafael just dominates every conversation so I didn't speak a lot. It wasn't very useful for me because I didn't practice speaking.

Tuesday 22nd _____

[ ] Great class today. We finished reading a novel last
[ ] week and today the teacher gave us some fun questions to answer. I got 20/25 correct—not bad! Then we had to write two or three paragraphs about the entire story. That was difficult because the story is a little complicated and I didn't know how to put all the information into a short text.

Wednesday 23rd _____

[ ] The most boring class today—about credit and
[ ] inflation and a hundred other things I don't understand. And I have to write 2,000 words on the causes of the global recession for Wed. 30th. I hate this class!

Thursday 24th _____

[ ] Cool! We're going to look at different kinds of electricity
[ ] —static, electro-magnetic, etc. And then we are going to find some practical applications for it. Finally, something useful in school! The only problem is that we have to do it with a partner, and I have to work with Jordan – she talks a lot!.

Friday 25th _____

[ ] Oh great! Fantastic! The perfect way to finish the week
[ ] —one hour sitting in silence answering stupid algebra questions. Did you know that $2/x = (3 \times y - 2)$? No? I didn't either and I don't think I will ever need to use it. And then we have to write a journal entry about what we've learned! But I guess I didn't learn anything! OMG!

2 Reread the journal and match these subjects to the days. There's one extra subject.

chemistry   economics   ~~foreign languages~~
literature   mathematics   physics

3 Order the words in a–d to make questions. Reread the journal and answer them.

a Carrie / why / pollution / talk / about / didn't / ?
b she / exercise / enjoy / Tuesday / did / what / on / ?
c long / have / paper / write / does / she / to / how / the / ?
d bad / was / Thursday / about / what / ?

4 ◉ 5.3 Complete the quiz with *can't / don't have to / have to*. Listen to check.

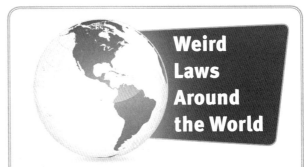

a You _____ drive a dirty car in Russia.
b In Bolivia, Paraguay, and Peru you _____ have permission to get married at 16.
c You _____ buy chewing gum in Singapore.
d You _____ have a license to have a dog in Canada.
e You _____ have a TV without a license in the United Kingdom.
f You _____ carry an ID card in the U.S.
g Citizens _____ participate in elections in Chile and Venezuela.
h In Brazil men _____ register for military service in the year of their 18th birthday. Women _____ register, but they can if they want to.

5 ◉ 5.4 Follow the model.

Model: *Obligation. I / work / on Saturday.*
You: *I have to work on Saturday.*
Model: *No obligation.*
You: *I don't have to work on Saturday.*
Model: *My brother.*
You: *My brother doesn't have to work on Saturday.*

6 🎤 **Make it personal** Which laws in 4 would you find most difficult to live with? Why?

5.3 Are you a good student?

1 ▶5.5 **Make it personal** Match a–e to 1–5 to make advice for students. Listen to check and write two more pieces of advice.

a Be enthusiastic about what you are learning. When you are…

b If you want to optimize your classes, you can download material about the topic in…

c You will have to do a lot of reading, so find a good online dictionary so you can look…

d Don't miss too many classes! You can use the college portal to find…

e If the schoolwork is too much for you, don't drop…

1 out. Of course college can be difficult, but talk to your teacher, we are here to help.

2 out exactly where they are and what time they start and store the info on your phone planner.

3 really into a topic it's a lot easier to learn.

4 advance. You will benefit a lot more if you already understand a little about the topic of each lesson.

5 up new academic words and then use them when you write a paper.

2 Complete song lines a–d with *too* or *enough*.

a "You've got a fast car. But is it fast _____ so we can fly away? We've got to make a decision. We leave tonight or live and die this way." Tracy Chapman

b "I called up my congressman and he said, quote: 'I'd like to help you son but you're _____ young to vote.'" Eddie Cochran

c "_____ many people going underground. _____ many reaching for a piece of cake." Paul McCartney

d "Ain't no mountain high _____, ain't no valley low _____, ain't no river wide _____ to keep me from getting to you, baby." Marvin Gaye and Tammi Terrel

3 Order the words in a–h to make sentences and match two of them to each picture 1–4.

a don't / enough / we / gasoline / have / .
b been / there's / rain / much / too .
c big / the / shirt / isn't / enough / .
d it's / away / far / too / .
e boats / enough / aren't / there .
f heavy / is / him / suitcase / the / too / for / .
g too / to / the / the / man / suitcase / is / lift / weak / .
h eaten / food / much / he's / too .

4 Complete the captions for pictures a–d.

a I'm tired. This is _too_ much exercise for me.
b I don't want to get in line. There _____ many _____.

c Give me the keys. You're _____ old _____ to drive.
d I _____ have _____ to buy a phone.

5 ▶5.6 Listen, then circle the /ʌ/ sounds and underline the /uː/ sounds in the bold letters. Notice the different spellings.

a D**o** y**ou** have en**ou**gh f**u**n in sch**oo**l?
b Bl**ue** ch**ew**ing g**u**m isn't good f**oo**d.
c Do y**ou** know s**o**meone wh**o** has t**oo** m**u**ch m**o**ney?

/ʌ/
/uː/

6 **Make it personal** Write your answers to questions a and c in **5**.

26

5.4 What will you do when you pass this course?

1 ▶5.7 **Use the pictures and these phrases to complete the man's excuse. Listen to check.**

divorce   get jealous   ~~get up~~   go out   ~~go to work~~   meet my friends

> I'm not getting out of bed today. If I do, you'll divorce me.

> If I get up, I'll go to work. And if I go to work...

2 **Match the columns to make travel questions.**

a If I take cash in our currency with me,

b Will the airline give me a hotel room

c Will my laptop be OK

☐ if I take it with me?

☐ will I be able to change it when I arrive?

☐ if my flight is canceled?

3 **Circle the correct option, then match the answers to questions a–c in 2.**

☐ The airline will **to help** / **help** you if there is a problem with the plane.

☐ Don't put it in your suitcase. If you do, you probably **will** / **won't** see it again.

☐ Probably yes. But if you **will take** / **take** some US dollars or Euros, you'll be safe.

☐ If the the flight **is** / **will be** canceled because of the weather, you probably won't get a hotel.

☐ If you **will travel** / **are traveling** by plane, you can carry it with you.

4 **Order the words in a–d to make travel tips.**

a Put your hotel's phone number in your cell phone. them / you / if / call / lost / get / .

b you / close / bus / the / by / door / travel / if / sit / to / . It's easier to get on and off with your bags.

c shy / someone / don't / talks / if / to / you / be / ! You can learn a lot from a conversation with a local person.

d speak / if / the / don't / don't / worry / you / language / . You can communicate a lot with gestures.

5 **Rewrite a–g as zero (0) or first (1st) conditionals.**

a (1st) rain / I use / umbrella. *If it rains, I'll use an umbrella.*

b (0) you / not have / passport / you / not can / go abroad. _____

c (1st) I take vacation / I / go / beach. _____

d (0) I feel sick / I eat too many cupcakes. _____

e (0) you travel / you learn new things. _____

f (1st) your vacation / be great / it be sunny. _____

g (1st) What / you do / it snow? _____

6 ▶5.8 **Listen to check. Repeat the sentences after the beep and copy the intonation.**

7 🎧 **Make it personal** Write five pieces of advice to someone traveling to another country for the first time?

5.5 How do you usually get in touch?

1 **Read the blog post and replace the underlined words with the correct pronoun or possessive adjective.**

Paula's blog Mothers and Technology

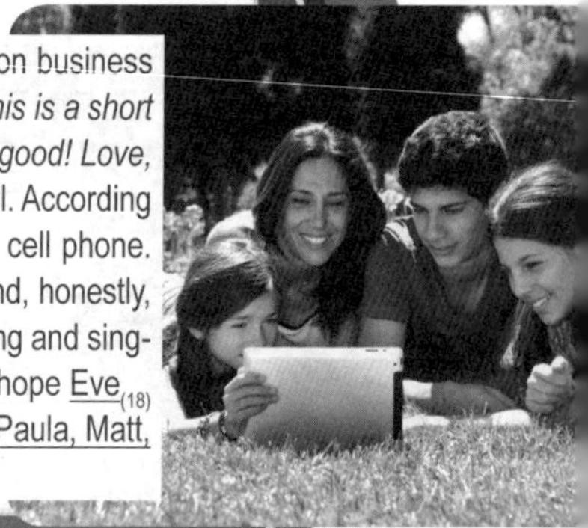

~~Paula's~~ My children all have e-mail addresses now, even Paula's(1) nine-year-old, so when Paula(2) was away on business last week Paula(3) decided to embrace technology. Paula(4) sent the children(5) a group e-mail: *Hi darlings! This is a short message to say I'll be home on Saturday and I'm really excited about seeing you all. I hope you are being good! Love, Mom.* Matt, 17, didn't reply. Matt(6) only communicates on Facebook and Twitter and Matt(7) never uses e-mail. According to Matt(8), e-mail(9) is "*last century*." Anna, 15, occasionally uses e-mail, but Anna(10) checks it on Anna's(11) cell phone. Eve, 9, replied immediately: *hi m! luv u.* There were no capital letters and the spelling was very strange and, honestly, Paula(12) was a little disappointed. The rest of the e-mail was full of small yellow faces – the faces(13) were dancing and singing. Paula(14) had never seen the faces(15) before so Paula(16) learned something from Paula's(17) daughter. I hope Eve(18) will learn spelling from Paula(19)! But although technology gives me, Matt, Anna and Eve(20) some problems, Paula, Matt, Anna and Eve(21) can still communicate face-to-face – real communication, so I'm pleased about that.

2 **Re-read and answer a–e True (T), False (F), or Not mentioned (N).**

a Paula usually sends group emails to her children.
b All of her children replied.
c Paula doesn't mind if her children use cyber English.
d Animated emoticons are new to Paula.
e Paula's happy because her children talk to her.

3 **5.9 Listen and order the pictures, 1–6.**

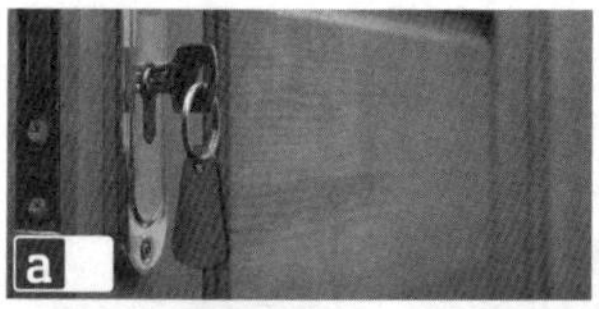
a
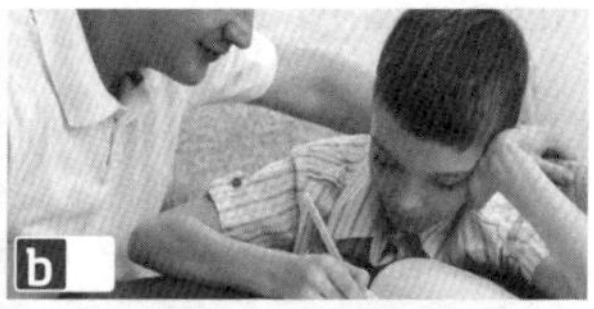
b
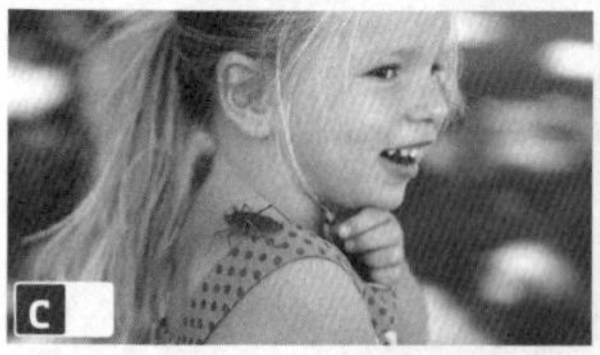
c
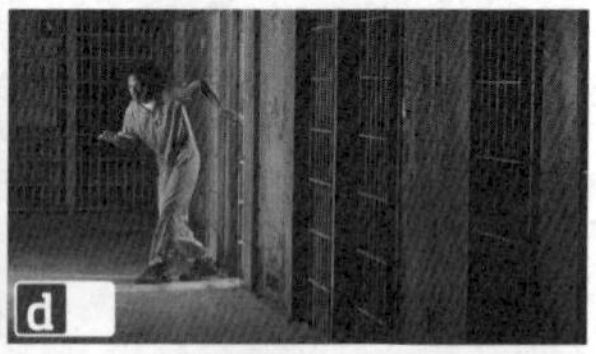
d
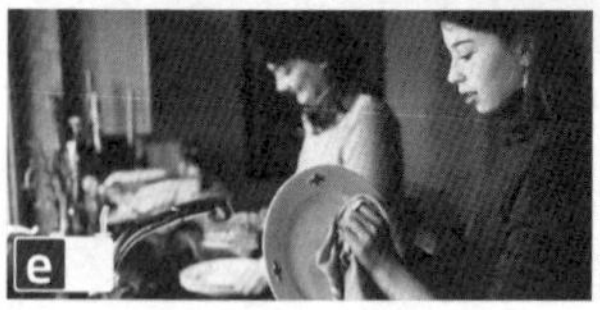
e
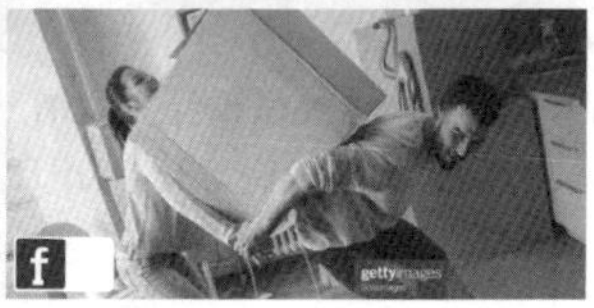
f

4 **5.9 Complete a–f. Listen again to check and repeat after the beep.**

a ______ out! If you ______ ______ ______ they'll hear you!
b Be careful. If you drop it, ______ ______.
c Don't ______! ______ ______ something on your back.
d Whatever you do, ______ ______ ______ lock the door.
e I'll do the dishes ______ ______ ______ ______ with my homework.
f If you ______ ______ ______, I'll take you out to eat.

5 **Make it personal** **Make your own promises. Complete a–d and email them to a friend.**

a If you help me with my homework, ______________.
b If you lend me some money, ______________.
c If you buy me a coffee, ______________.
d I'll love you forever if ______________.

6 **5.10** **Make it personal** **Listen and match questions a–e to the answers. Then write or record your own answers.**

a Why did you choose this school?
b What did you do at school today?
c What advice can you give to a new student?
d Do you ever make terrible excuses?
e Do you send a lot of emails in English?

☐ Uh, I guess "make an effort" is good advice.
☐ I can't remember. Oh, yes! We started a project in chemistry class.
☐ No, not many. But I send a few texts now and then.
☐ I didn't choose it. It's just the closest to my house.
☐ No, I'm pretty honest, so I just tell the truth.

Connect

Write a short tweet with your advice.

Can you remember ...

- 18 school subjects? SB→p. 58
- 10 class activities? SB→p. 60
- the difference between *have to, don't have to* and *can't*? SB→p. 61
- which is correct — *miss* or *lose a class*? SB→p. 62
- how to use *too* and *enough* with adjectives? SB→p. 63
- 2 sentence structures with *if*? SB→p. 64
- 6 phrases to use with warnings? SB→p. 67

6.1 Have you ever been to Florida?

1 ▶6.1 Practice the picture words and a–e. Then listen to check your pronunciation.

a   I'm going shopping tomorrow morning.
b   We go clubbing every Friday evening.
c   I went swimming and diving last weekend.
d   We're going fishing next spring.
e   Let's go bowling in Washington!

/ɪ/

2 Complete the posts with these verbs in the correct form. Add *go* or *went* if necessary.

bowl   camp   climb   club   dive   fish   hang out   ~~hike~~   work out

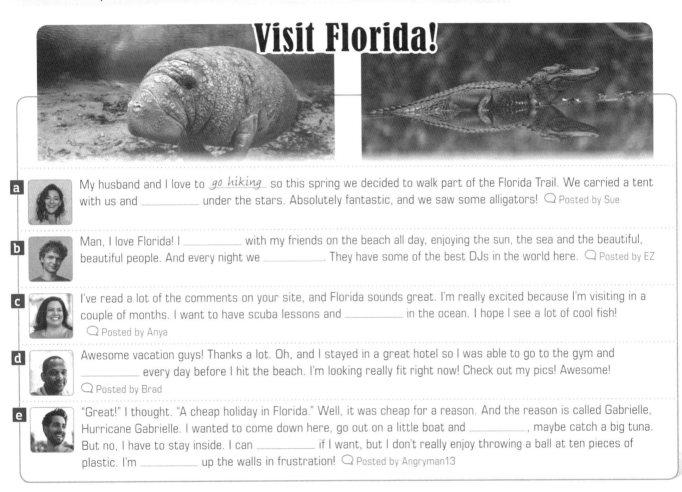

Visit Florida!

a   My husband and I love to *go hiking* so this spring we decided to walk part of the Florida Trail. We carried a tent with us and _____ under the stars. Absolutely fantastic, and we saw some alligators! ⚲ Posted by Sue

b   Man, I love Florida! I _____ with my friends on the beach all day, enjoying the sun, the sea and the beautiful, beautiful people. And every night we _____. They have some of the best DJs in the world here. ⚲ Posted by EZ

c   I've read a lot of the comments on your site, and Florida sounds great. I'm really excited because I'm visiting in a couple of months. I want to have scuba lessons and _____ in the ocean. I hope I see a lot of cool fish!
⚲ Posted by Anya

d   Awesome vacation guys! Thanks a lot. Oh, and I stayed in a great hotel so I was able to go to the gym and _____ every day before I hit the beach. I'm looking really fit right now! Check out my pics! Awesome!
⚲ Posted by Brad

e   "Great!" I thought. "A cheap holiday in Florida." Well, it was cheap for a reason. And the reason is called Gabrielle, Hurricane Gabrielle. I wanted to come down here, go out on a little boat and _____, maybe catch a big tuna. But no, I have to stay inside. I can _____ if I want, but I don't really enjoy throwing a ball at ten pieces of plastic. I'm _____ up the walls in frustration! ⚲ Posted by Angryman13

3 Reread and answer a–e.
a   Which two people mention the weather?
b   Which person is writing about a future vacation?
c   Which two went on vacation with friends or relatives?
d   Which person is happy with their body?
e   Is Angryman13 really climbing up the walls?

4 🎧 **Make it personal** Write your answers to the questions.
1   Which experience, a–e in **2**, would you most like to try? Why?
2   Are there any you definitely wouldn't like to try? Why not?
3   Have you ever had any similar experiences? What happened?

📶 **Connect**
Record your answers on your phone. Send them to a classmate or your teacher.

6.2 Would you like to try hang gliding?

1 Read the blog posts and label the photos with the names.

Travel blog spot 🔍 Baños

I had a cool experience in Baños. There are a few tour companies that organize "canyoning" trips. Basically you just climb _____ waterfalls, but it is so exhilarating as the water rushes past you.
On the trip I went on, we climbed three waterfalls. The first was only about five meters, but the final one was giant—35 meters down! One piece of advice, wear gloves 'cause the rope can hurt your hands.
Posted 29 November by Frederico

Amazing day in Baños! We went white-water rafting _____ the Pastaza river. OMG! I have never been so terrified. At one point I thought the raft was going to turn over and leave us all in the river. Apparently, the rapids are usually a class two, but the water level was unusually high so some parts were class five rapids—there are only six classes! Anyway, although it was scary it was also really fun. I would recommend it to anyone.
Posted 29 July by Heitor

After a week of hiking in the mountains, Baños was a welcome relief for my aching muscles. This Ecuadorean town is full of hot spas, that are heated by the local volcano! The spas range from around 18°C to 55°C and are full of natural minerals. After a couple of days submerged _____ the hot water and then jumping _____ the refreshing cold water pools, my legs feel ready for the next challenge. Bring on the mountains!
Posted 10 February by Jillian

2 ▶6.2 Complete the posts with the words in the box. Listen to check.

down   in   into   on

3 Reread and complete a–c.
a If you go canyoning, wear _____ to protect your _____.
b The rapids were class five because the _____ was _____.
c Jillian was _____ in the _____ before she arrived in Baños.

4 Use clues a–h to make compound nouns and complete the puzzle.
a coffee / World – c u p
b pass / air / computer – __ __ __ __
c class / living / bed – __ __ __ __
d news / toilet / sand – __ __ __ __ __
e skate / surf – __ __ __ __
f __ __ __ – glasses / bathing
g __ __ __ __ – bag / ball / shake
h __ __ __ __ __ – son / father / mother

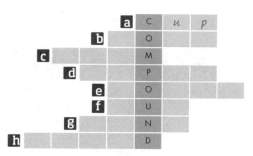

5 Label these pictures with words from the puzzle.

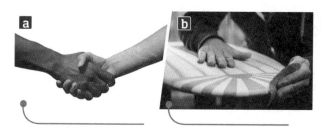

6 Complete the verbs of movement with the missing letters.
a d _ v _   e f _ ll
b r _ n   f sw _ m
c sn _ wb _ _ rd   g cl _ mb
d j _ mp

7 😀 **Make it personal** Write your answers to the questions.
1 Would you like to visit Baños? Why (not)?
2 Which of the experiences in **1** would you most like to try? Why?

30

6.3 Do you feel like going out tonight?

1 Look at the pictures and complete extracts *a* and *b* with the correct prepositions.

a over   under   ~~along~~   towards   into   out of

It's very easy, really. At first you run _along_ the course, _____ the big wall. Then you climb _____ the wall and jump _____ the big pool of mud on the other side. Once you get _____ the mud pool, it's just straight _____ the electric fence and then the bridge.

b up   down   past   across

Last night I went to the movies. While I was waiting for the movie to start, I looked _____ the theater and saw an old school friend walking _____ the steps. She didn't see me and walked straight _____ me then sat _____ in her seat. I wanted to call out to her, but then it went quiet and the movie started.

2 ▶6.3 Match a–g to 1–7. Listen to check.
a During school vacations, I really miss …
b I have exams this year, so I have to start …
c I haven't finished …
d I want to practice …
e I'm a great student, but my teacher keeps …
f I really can't stand …
g I don't feel like …

1 giving me bad grades. I don't know why.
2 waiting for the bus. I'm too impatient!
3 studying seriously if I want to pass.
4 seeing my school buddies every day.
5 cooking tonight. Let's order some pizza.
6 listening, so I rented a movie in English.
7 reading that book yet. Don't tell me the end!

3 Make pairs with similar meanings. Check the strongest in each pair.
a adore
b beautiful
c large
d dislike
e funny

☐ can't stand
☐ enjoy
☐ hilarious
☐ pretty
☐ huge

4 🅐 **Make it personal** Use the verbs in 3 and the prompts to make true sentences.
a I _enjoy cooking_ (cook).
b My mom _____ (clean the house).
c I _____ (go clubbing).
d My best friend _____ (shop).
e I _____ (travel long distances).
f I _____ (work out).

5 ▶6.4 Say sentences a–c and listen to check your pronunciation. Notice the voiced /ð/ and unvoiced /θ/. Then match the bold words to pictures 1 and 2 and answer question b.
a I'll always be **there**, **with** or **without** you.
b Who is my **father**'s **brother**'s **mother**'s grandchild?
c She **threw the toothbrush through** the window.

6.4 What do you enjoy doing on your birthday?

1 Complete definitions a–e with prepositions and match them to the sports.

baseball   scuba diving   soccer   swimming   volleyball

a Use a mask and an oxygen tank to swim ___under___ the water. You can wear fins to swim more efficiently.

b Use your arms and legs to move _____ the water. You don't need any equipment.

c Use your hands to hit a ball _____ a net. There are six people on each team and the first to win three sets of 25 points wins.

d Use a bat to hit a ball and then run _____ the bases. Players on the other team will try to catch the ball and they wear gloves for protection. If they catch the ball, you're out.

e Use your feet to kick a ball _____ a goal. One player on each team can use their hands to stop the ball.

2 Underline eight different pieces of equipment in the descriptions in **1**.

3 ▶ 6.5 Read the dialogue and circle the correct form. Listen to check.

Harry You look nervous Liz. Are you OK?
Liz Yeah, I'm OK. It's just that I have this job interview tomorrow, for the sports instructor job, and I'm a little nervous. Can I practice **to interview / interviewing** with you?
Harry Sure, I guess. So, Liz, why did you decide **to be / being** a sports instructor?
Liz OK. So first, I really enjoy **to work out / working out** and, second, I want **to help / helping** other people get in shape. I think health and fitness are very important.
Harry Good answer. OK, next question. Why would you like **to join / joining** our team?
Liz Well, I know that you have very good facilities here and I hope **to learn / learning** a lot about the business.
Harry OK, great! A personal question now. What's the most difficult thing you have ever done?
Liz Um, I don't know. Oh! I quit **to smoke / smoking** three years ago. That was very difficult. My boyfriend agreed **to quit / quitting** smoking with me, but he couldn't do it. He still smokes—stupid him!
Harry Thanks! OK, final question. What kind of salary are you expecting?
Liz Well, I've done some research and I expect **to make / making** between $26,000 and $30,000.
Harry Liz, you sounded very confident, you're going to do great! Just don't forget **to relax / relaxing**.

4 ▶ 6.6 Follow the model. Practice the sentences.
Model: would like / go to the party   **Model:** enjoy / play sports
You: I'd like to go to the party.   **You:** I enjoy playing sports.

5 🅐 **Make it personal** Complete a–f with **to study** or **studying** and circle the best option to make the sentences true for you.
a I **will / won't** keep _____ English after this book.
b I decided _____ English because **I like it / I need it**.
c I'**d like / don't want** _____ another language after this.
d My teacher **asked / didn't ask** me _____ English this weekend.
e I **often / don't often** forget _____ on weekends.
f I **enjoy / don't enjoy** _____ on my own.

Connect
Interview your partner about what they like doing on their birthday and record it on your phone.

32

6.5 Would you rather stay in or go out?

1 Read and match the highlighted words to items a–c in the photo.

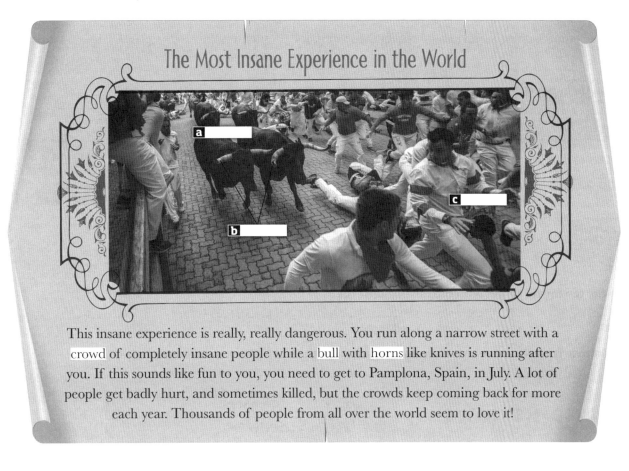

The Most Insane Experience in the World

This insane experience is really, really dangerous. You run along a narrow street with a crowd of completely insane people while a bull with horns like knives is running after you. If this sounds like fun to you, you need to get to Pamplona, Spain, in July. A lot of people get badly hurt, and sometimes killed, but the crowds keep coming back for more each year. Thousands of people from all over the world seem to love it!

2 ▶6.7 Listen to interviews 1–4. Who has run with the bulls?

3 ▶6.7 Who said these things? Listen again and match.
1 Shane ☐ I guess …
2 Petra ☐ … you know?
3 Jake ☐ Not in a million years!
4 Lucia ☐ It looks really crazy.

4 ▶6.8 Order dialogues *a* and *b*. Listen to check.
a At home
☐ M I don't feel like watching a movie. Let's go and see the band.
☐ W It's OK, but I've seen it before. I'll turn it off.
☐ M So, what do you want to do this evening?
☐ W Hmm, I don't know. Do you want to go to the movies? Or, there's a band playing.
☐ M I'm bored with this program, aren't you?

b At the bar
☐ W No thanks. I'm on an alcohol-free diet.
☐ M OK, one orange juice coming up.
☐ W Would you like a drink?
☐ W Uh, I'd rather have an orange juice, please.
☐ M Oh. So, how about a Coke?
☐ M It's OK, I'll get it. Would you like a beer?

5 ▶6.9 Listen to the end of the dialogue and fill in each blank with two words.
The man didn't like the band. He _____ to _____.
The woman liked the band. She _____ to _____ again.

Can you remember …
▶ 9 leisure time activities? SB→p. 72
▶ 5 extreme sports? SB→p. 74
▶ 5 verb / adverbial preposition combinations? SB→p. 75
▶ 5 common compound nouns? SB→p. 75
▶ 12 prepositions of movement? SB→p. 76
▶ 8 verbs that are followed by -ing? SB→p. 76
▶ 11 pieces of sports equipment? SB→p. 78
▶ 5 sports verbs? SB→p. 78
▶ 7 verbs that are followed by *to* + infinitive? SB→p. 79

7

7.1 How often do you go to the movies?

1 Read the funny definitions and complete them with the words in the box.

> box office   stunt   plot   review   sequel   soundtrack   subtitles

Diabolical Definitions!

a _____ *noun* [C] when you have to pay twice to see one story.

b _____ *noun* [C] something a brave (or just stupid) person does.

c _____ *noun* [C] a place where you pay a lot of money and get a small piece of paper.

d _____ *noun* [C] something you read if you want to talk about the movie but don't want to watch it.

e _____ *noun* [C] things that allow you to talk to friends and understand the movie at the same time.

f _____ *noun* [C] a series of increasingly incredible events that you have to believe.

g _____ *noun* [C] if you can't remember the story, maybe you'll remember the music.

It's your fault.

2 Complete the ten movie genres with the missing letters.

a m_____y   c _n_m___d   e ____l__r   g __r__r   i c___d_
b __a_a   d a____n   f d___m_____   h __v__t___   j ___t_s_

3 Read three movie reviews and match them to the genre and the stars. There is one extra genre.

▶ Movie Reviews

☐ Comedy   ☐ Gangster
☐ Sci-Fi   ☐ Suspense

a ★
b ★★★
c ★★★★★

1 At 158 minutes, this movie is about 150 minutes too long. It starts well and there are some genuine laughs in the opening sequence, but after that it gets worse. This was not as funny as the first movie, let's hope that the next in the series isn't a disappointment too.

2 I don't usually enjoy this actor, so when I bought my ticket at the box office I wasn't expecting a lot, but I have to say this movie really impressed me. The plot slowly increases the tension through the entire movie and I couldn't guess the ending at all. It is a very intelligent story with some superb acting.

3 This is the story of Danny's fight to the top against his rivals in crime. The violence is sometimes very strong—don't watch this movie if you are sensitive to blood. The plot is a little predictable but there are also some emotional scenes, for example, when Danny discovers that his brother is a traitor working for the police. Danny's reaction is inevitable and is also the cause of his ruin.

4 Reread and answer a–e. Which movie ...

a   is good at the start?   c   was surprisingly good?   e   is a sequel?
b   had an unpredictable story?   d   is probably not good for young children?

5 Correct two mistakes in each of a–c.

a   The *Terminator 2* is one old movie starring Arnold Schwarzenegger.
b   The most actors want to win the Oscar.
c   I watched a great movie on the TV the last night.

6 🎧 **Make it personal**   Complete the review about a movie you have seen. You can expand this short review if you have more to say.

> The last movie I saw was _____ (name). It's a _____ (genre) movie starring _____ (actor). I **liked / didn't like** it because it is _____ (adjective). I **would / wouldn't** recommend it to you.

34

7.2 Are you crazy about music?

1 Choose the best word / phrase to complete the sentences.

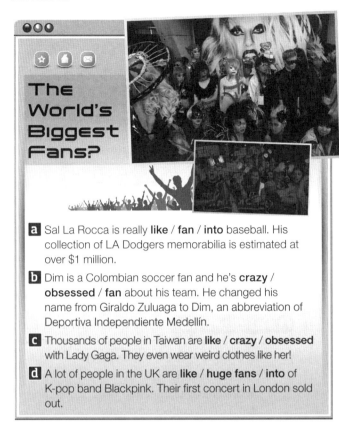

a Sal La Rocca is really **like** / **fan** / **into** baseball. His collection of LA Dodgers memorabilia is estimated at over $1 million.

b Dim is a Colombian soccer fan and he's **crazy** / **obsessed** / **fan** about his team. He changed his name from Giraldo Zuluaga to Dim, an abbreviation of Deportiva Independiente Medellín.

c Thousands of people in Taiwan are **like** / **crazy** / **obsessed** with Lady Gaga. They even wear weird clothes like her!

d A lot of people in the UK are **like** / **huge fans** / **into** of K-pop band Blackpink. Their first concert in London sold out.

2 Cross out the word that doesn't fit the group.

a video / DVD / ~~photo~~
b earrings / sunglasses / haircut
c general public / paparazzi / journalist
d huge / really / very
e love / adore / obsessed

3 Complete the sentences with *some*, *any*, *every* or *no*.

a There's _____ thing we can do about this, it's impossible to fix.
b I've never met _____ one like you before.
c Can I have _____ thing to eat, please? I'm hungry.
d We asked _____ body, but _____ body knows anything, I'm afraid.
e We need to find _____ one for the job.
f You can sit _____ where you want.

4 ▶ 7.1 Read the story and circle the correct word. Listen to check.

My Birthday

I got up in the morning and checked the mail. There were some letters for my parents, but there was **nothing** / **something** for me.

I got to work and said "Hi" to my colleagues, but **no one** / **anyone** said **nothing** / **anything** to me.

At lunch, I went to the cafeteria. It was very busy and there wasn't **nowhere** / **anywhere** to sit. I had to wait for **someone** / **anyone** to finish his food before I could sit down.

I was a little angry because I never forget **anyone's** / **everyone's** birthday and **anyone** / **everyone** was ignoring mine, so after work I went to the park to try and relax.

It was a beautiful sunny afternoon, and I tried to find **anywhere** / **somewhere** to sit, but it was very crowded and there were people **everywhere** / **somewhere**.

After dark, I drove home, but my street was full of cars and there was **anywhere** / **nowhere** for me to park my car. What a terrible day! **Everything** / **Anything** was going wrong.

I parked my car two streets from my house and walked home. There was **anything** / **something** very strange happening, but I didn't know what it was.

I arrived home and when I opened the door, I couldn't believe it. **Someone** / **Everyone** was there. It was a surprise birthday party, and they were all waiting for me!

🔊 Connect

Record yourself describing your last birthday on your phone, then send it to a classmate or your teacher.

5 ▶ 7.2 Circle the word where the bold letter has a different sound. Listen to check.

a s**o**mewhere   n**o**   n**o**thing
b **a**nything   **e**verything f**a**n
c n**o**where   **o**ne   **o**nly

6 🎧 **Make it personal** What did you do for your last birthday? Write a short story like the one in **4**.

35

7.3 What do you have a lot of at home?

1 Read and match a–d to their endings to complete the four world records. Then match them to photos 1–4.

Crazy World Records!

1 2 3 4

ⓐ Freddie is the world's tallest dog measuring 40.75 in. and weighing 196 lbs. He is so…

ⓑ The Insano in Fortaleza, Brazil, is the world's tallest waterslide: 41 meters. It has such…

ⓒ Kazuhiro Watanabe is in the world record books with the world's tallest Mohican. It took him 15 years to grow such…

ⓓ The Giant Weta is a kind of insect from New Zealand. In fact, it is the world's largest insect and, although its legs are designed for jumping, it is so…

- [ ][ ] … heavy that it can't jump!
- [ ][ ] … an impressive hairstyle.
- [ ][ ] … big that small children think he is a horse.
- [ ][ ] … a sudden fall that people can go up to 105 km/h before arriving in the pool.

2 Read and complete the diary with *so* or *such*. Add *a* or *an* if necessary.

Monday
My boss is _____¹ idiot. She made a lot of mistakes today and then she made me stay late to help her make everything right again!

Tuesday
There was _____² much traffic this morning that I arrived 30 minutes late. My boss looked a little angry but she didn't say anything because I helped her yesterday. HaHaHa!

Wednesday
Vicki and I wanted to go to the movies after work, but when we got to the mall the line for tickets was _____³ long that we decided to go shopping instead!

Thursday
Mario came to deliver some things to the office today. He is _____⁴ good-looking and he is _____⁵ friendly guy too. I have to find out if he has a girlfriend!

Friday
It was _____⁶ beautiful day that I went to the park at lunchtime. It was _____⁷ hot and I was _____⁸ tired that I fell asleep! Luckily I was back in the office before my boss.

3 ▶7.3 Make sentences with *so* or *such*. Follow the model.
Model: *He's lazy.* **Model:** *He's a good cook.*
You: *He's so lazy.* **You:** *He's such a good cook.*

4 🎙 **Make it personal** Write questions a–d. Each / means one word. Then choose the best answer for you and complete them if necessary.

a / / collect anything?
- [ ] Yeah, I have a collection of _____.
- [ ] No, I don't collect anything.

b / / into sports?
- [ ] Yeah, I love _____.
- [ ] No, I don't do any sports.

c / / have / favorite artist?
- [ ] I'm really into _____. I also like _____.
- [ ] No, I don't have a favorite.

d Which soccer team / / support?
- [ ] I'm a _____ fan.
- [ ] I don't like soccer.

📶 Connect

Interview your partner with the questions and record it on your phone.

5 ▶7.4 Listen to four dialogues. Complete follow-up questions a–d and match them to the answers.

a _____ do you have?
b _____ do you play?
c _____ seen her perform?
d Have you ever _____?

- [ ] Yeah, I went last year.
- [ ] Unfortunately, no, I haven't.
- [ ] About 50.
- [ ] About once a week.

7.4 Who was Instagram created by?

1 Read the introduction to the article. Is it about:
   a an animated movie?
   b a group of animated movies?

A Success STORY

Animated movies are becoming more and more sophisticated and often adults enjoy them as much as children do. In this article, we will look at one of the most popular and successful animated series of all time.

2 Read the rest of the article and cross out the incorrect verb form.

The **TOY STORY** series **is loved** / ~~loves~~ by children and adults all over the world and each of the three movies has received fantastic reviews globally too. The first movie **is released** / **was released** in 1995 and became the first movie to **create** / **be created** entirely with CGI (computer-generated imagery). In the movie, Andy **gets** / **is gotten** a new toy, Buzz Lightyear. The old toy, Woody, worries that Andy doesn't like him anymore.

TOY STORY 2 didn't intend / **wasn't intended** for the movie theaters. The original plan was for a short video sequel. However, the voice actors were so enthusiastic about the movie that they **persuaded** / **were persuaded** the executives to make a full movie. In this movie Woody **captures** / **is captured** by a toy collector and the other toys go on a mission to save him.

TOY STORY 3 was released in 2010, eleven years after **TOY STORY 2**. This movie **made** / **is made** more than $1 billion in the box office, the first animated movie to do so. In this movie Andy is leaving to go to college and his toys **accidently throw** / **are accidently thrown** in the garbage. The toys' adventures take them to a kindergarten, and a garbage truck before they **find** / **are found** Andy again.

In 2019, **TOY STORY 4** came out. In this fourth movie, the characters **joined** / **are joined** by Forky, a spork that Bonnie makes into a toy, and go on a road trip adventure. It has made even more money than **TOY STORY 3**, and is another wonderful movie full of humor and emotion!

MOVIE MAGAZINE | P. 101

3 ▶7.5 Listen and complete the statistics.
   a In total, the first three movies made $_____ worldwide.
   b The review website Rotten Tomatoes ranks the movies as the most acclaimed series ever. On average, the movies have a _____% positive review rates.
   c Toy Story 2 is the shortest in the series. It is a little over _____ hours.
   d The _____ movie had _____ new characters.
   e Toy Story 3 won _____ of the Oscars it was nominated for.
   f Toy Story 4 was released in theaters in the United States on June _____, 2019.

4 ▶7.6 Write complete sentences in the past passive. Then listen to check. Mark the participles regular (R) or irregular (I).
   a Game of Thrones / write / George R. R. Martin
   b "Live it up", the official song of the 2018 World Cup, / sing / Nicky Jam featuring Will Smith & Era Istrefi
   c The World Wide Web / invent / Tim Berners-Lee
   d Microsoft / found / Bill Gates and Paul Allen

5 ▶7.7 Listen to the sound of -ed + a in sentences a-f. Do you hear (1) /də/ or (2) /dɪdə/?
   a He downloa<u>ded a</u> movie. 2   c They play<u>ed a</u> game.   e They stu<u>died a</u> book.
   b They design<u>ed a</u> car.   d She foun<u>ded a</u> company.   f The scientists captur<u>ed a</u> monster.

6 🎤 Make it personal What are your three favorite movies? Why do you like them? Record your answers.

7.5 Are you a good singer?

1 ▶ 7.8 Listen and match these words to the pictures according to the sound of the <u>underlined</u> letters.

> audition   catch   church   conclu<u>s</u>ion
> deci<u>s</u>ion   expre<u>ss</u>ion   illu<u>s</u>ion   kit<u>ch</u>en
> participa<u>t</u>ion   pronuncia<u>t</u>ion
> ques<u>t</u>ion   <u>sh</u>ow

/ʃ/ shorts, shark, audition
/tʃ/ cheese, chair

/ʒ/ treasure, television

2 ▶ 7.8 Listen again and mark the stress in 1. Can you notice a stress pattern in -ion words?

3 ▶ 7.9 Order the words in a–c to make questions. Then listen and answer.
 a is / on / watching / what / TV / Jess / ?
 b show / the / Helen / like / does / ?
 c nervous / does / Helen / why / feel / ?

4 ▶ 7.9 Listen again and count how many times you hear these expressions.
 ☐ As I was saying   ☐ Anyway   ☐ You know

5 ▶ 7.10 Make a–c more tactful. Listen to check.

 [a] I expected the movie to be good. In fact, it was terrible! I'm really disappointed!
   _____ wasn't as _____ as _____.

 [b] Everyone says the soundtrack is great! I thought it was absolutely awful!
   _____ didn't _____ all that great.

 [c] I didn't think the movie was terrible, but it certainly wasn't fantastic.
   Well, _____ OK, but not really five stars.

6 🔒 **Make it personal** Complete sentences a–c. Use these ideas to help you.

> a book   a movie   a place
> a restaurant   a sporting event

 a I **thought** / **didn't think** _____ was **great** / **interesting** / **fun**.
 b I thought _____ was OK, but nothing special.
 c _____ **was** / **wasn't** as **good** / **interesting** / **useful** / **fun** as I expected.

7 ▶ 7.11 🔒 **Make it personal** Listen and match questions a–e to the answers. Then write or record your own answers. Add more details too.
 a Do you ever download movies?
 b What's the last movie you saw?
 c Did you like the last movie you saw?
 d Do you have any posters in your room?
 e What do you collect?

 ☐ I collect money from different countries.
 ☐ Yeah, I have an old Spider-Man poster from when I was younger.
 [a] Sometimes, but my Internet connection is kind of slow.
 ☐ I watched a horror movie on TV last night.
 ☐ It was OK, but it was a little predictable.

8 Rewrite the sentences using *such*.
 a The place was so noisy.
   It _____.
 b My car is so slow.
   I have _____.
 c The movie was so disappointing.
   It _____.
 d The documentary was very interesting.
   It _____.
 e The radio station is very popular.
   It _____.
 f Her collection of chairs is so strange.
   She has _____.

Can you remember ...
▶ 10 movie genres? SB→p. 86
▶ 6 movie words? SB→p. 87
▶ 6 ways to talk about your passion? SB→p. 88
▶ 3 compounds with -*thing*? SB→p. 89
▶ present and past ⊕⊖ *be* + past participle? SB→p. 93
▶ 3 ways to improve your speaking fluency? SB→p. 94
▶ 3 ways to give your opinion politely? SB→p. 95

8.1 Are you into science fiction?

1 Complete the sentences with *at*, *in* or *on*.
a Neil Armstrong was the first man on the moon _____ 02:56 GMT _____ July 21, 1969.
b The first email was sent _____ October 1971.
c The first Twitter message was "just setting up my twttr" and was posted _____ 09:50 PST _____ March 21, 2006.
d Facebook started _____ 2004.

2 Read the article and use the <u>underlined</u> phrases to write descriptions of the inventions.
<u>A door that can lock itself</u> = *A self-locking door*

New Inventions

a _____
Nobody likes waking up to the sound of an alarm clock beeping angrily at them in the morning. That's why this <u>alarm clock that can produce smells</u> provides a much nicer experience. You can wake up to the smell of freshly-baked bread, for example, or peppermint.

b _____
This amazing development allows you to heat your lunch without a kitchen. It connects to an app on your phone, and when you tell it to, the <u>lunch box can heat itself</u>, and your lunch. You can take it to work or when you go camping, and enjoy delicious hot food wherever you are.

c _____
A 17-year-old developer from London has released his fourth smartphone application (app). He started writing apps when he was 12 and now has his own company, but he still goes to school and he has exams to worry about. The new <u>app summarizes news</u> stories so that users can read news more easily on their smartphones.

3 Reread the article. True (T), False (F) or Not mentioned (N)?
a The alarm clock makes an angry beeping noise.
b People can choose the smell they want to wake up to.
c The food in the lunch box doesn't need to be cooked in an oven.
d The teenage software developer was born in London.
e The young inventor has dropped out of school.

🔗 Connect
Look up new inventions online and choose your favorite one.

4 Match words / phrases a–g to definitions 1–7.
a smart vending machine
b GPS
c surveillance camera
d a button
e facial recognition device
f speaker
g active contact lenses

1 Something that records video in order to help with security.
2 You can buy something from this device, which has a touch screen.
3 Something which produces sound.
4 Something you press on a machine.
5 Things which help you see and are connected to a computer.
6 A system that helps you use software maps in real time.
7 A special camera which recognizes your face.

5 Complete the sentences with one missing word.
a Welcome to the Happy Days Hotel. If you're hungry in the night we have a range of smart _____ machines which sell food.
b I think we're lost. Switch on your _____ so we can find the way.
c Sit near the _____ and you'll hear the music better.
d These active contact _____ make it much easier to see.
e My new cell phone uses a _____ recognition device to unlock it.

6 🎧 **Make it personal** Number the items below, 1–4, and do the same with all the pictures on this page.
1 I use it every day.
2 I use it more than once a week.
3 I use it more than once a month.
4 I have never used it.

☐ contact lenses
☐ a button on a remote control
☐ a surveillance camera
☐ a vending machine
☐ speaker
☐ a facial recognition device

8.2 Do you ever switch off from technology?

1 Study these sentences from ID **2**. Match phrasal verbs a–g with their definitions.

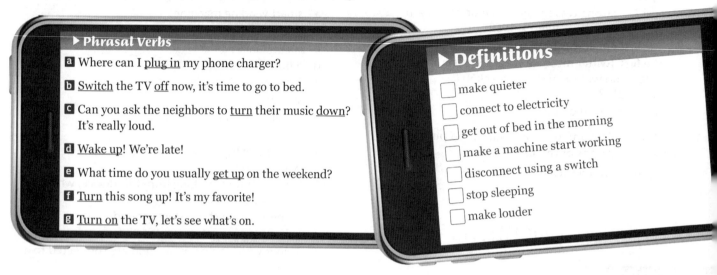

▶ **Phrasal Verbs**
a Where can I <u>plug in</u> my phone charger?
b <u>Switch</u> the TV <u>off</u> now, it's time to go to bed.
c Can you ask the neighbors to <u>turn</u> their music <u>down</u>? It's really loud.
d <u>Wake up</u>! We're late!
e What time do you usually <u>get up</u> on the weekend?
f <u>Turn</u> this song up! It's my favorite!
g <u>Turn on</u> the TV, let's see what's on.

▶ **Definitions**
☐ make quieter
☐ connect to electricity
☐ get out of bed in the morning
☐ make a machine start working
☐ disconnect using a switch
☐ stop sleeping
☐ make louder

2 Match a–d to their continuations 1–4.

a Shall we go out tonight?
b Can you pick up my bag please? Sorry, I can't reach.
c Put on your hat, it's sunny outside.
d Everyone stand up, please.

1 OK. Let me just take my hairband off first.
2 No, I'm tired. Let's just stay in and watch a movie.
3 Now find your partner and sit down next to them.
4 Sure. Where shall I put it down?

3 ▶ 8.1 Listen to phrases a–d in **2** then read the correct phrase, 1–4, after the beep.

4 Read the instruction manual and label the diagram with the bold words. Then complete the instructions with *down*, *on*, *off* or *up*.

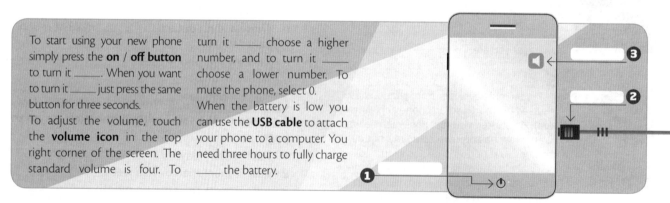

To start using your new phone simply press the **on / off button** to turn it ____. When you want to turn it ____ just press the same button for three seconds.
To adjust the volume, touch the **volume icon** in the top right corner of the screen. The standard volume is four. To turn it ____ choose a higher number, and to turn it ____ choose a lower number. To mute the phone, select 0.
When the battery is low you can use the **USB cable** to attach your phone to a computer. You need three hours to fully charge ____ the battery.

5 ▶ 8.2 Order the words in a–f to make questions about the cell phone. Predict the intonation and add ↗ or ↘. Listen to check and write the answers.

a your / cell phone / is / new / that / ?

b buy / you / where / it / did / ?

c the / last / battery / how long / does / ?

d it / with / I / can / play / ?

e have / apps / you / do / how many / ?

f do / does / this / what / app / ?

6 🎧 **Make it personal** Write instructions on how to use an app on your cell phone.

📶 **Connect**
Send your instructions in **6** *to a friend. Can she / he understand them?*

8.3 Will space vacations be popular soon?

1 ▶8.3 Listen and match these words to the pictures according to the sound of the <u>underlined</u> letters.

| sy<u>nth</u>etic | telepa<u>th</u>y | ~~<u>th</u>at~~ | <u>th</u>e | <u>th</u>emselves | ~~<u>th</u>eory~~ | <u>th</u>ere |
| <u>th</u>ey | <u>th</u>ink | <u>th</u>irty | <u>th</u>is | <u>th</u>oughts | <u>th</u>ree | <u>th</u>rough |

/θ/

theory

/ð/

that

Remember, when you say "father" or "teeth" you need to touch your teeth with your tongue.
"Th" can be voiced /ð/ or unvoiced /θ/.
Touch your throat when you say "father" and "teeth." Can you feel the vibration in "father"?

2 Read these predictions and add the adverbs in parentheses in the right place.

▶ What will cell phones be like in the future?

a Cell phone software will *definitely* get better, but the design *probably* won't change a lot. (~~definitely~~ / ~~probably~~)

b We will be able to download personalities for our cell phones and will have celebrity voices to read our texts. (**probably / possibly**)

c There have been big developments in screen technology and this will continue. (**certainly**)

d I think governments and organizations will use cell phone technology to collect information about individuals. (**possibly**)

e We won't use cell phones in the future. Using microchip technology, we will be able to communicate through telepathy. (**probably / possibly**)

3 Use the prompts to write more predictions about cell phones.
  a Cell phones / have / bigger screens ✚ probably   *Cell phones will probably have bigger screens.*
  b Cell phones / can / clean themselves ✚ possibly _____
  c Cell phones / be / "phones" ✖ definitely _____
  d We / need to touch / the screens ✖ probably _____
  e Cell phones / can / recognize our voices ✚ certainly _____

4 ▶8.4 Correct the mistakes in a–f. Listen to check.
  a 3D TV will be common in five years?
  b Will have a World War 3?
  c Did we had homework from the last class?
  d Are we go to have a test this week?
  e Is going to be sunny this weekend?
  f Will we be able to talk with aliens one day?

5 ▶8.5 Listen and circle the answers to the questions in **4**. What else do the speakers say?
  a I think so.   I hope not.   (I don't think so.)   *Maybe in 10 years.*
  b I hope so.   I don't think so. I hope not.   _____
  c I think so.   I don't think so. I hope so.   _____
  d I hope so.   I hope not.   I think so.   _____
  e I hope not.   I think so.   I don't think so.   _____
  f I hope so.   I hope.   I hope not.   _____

6 ▶8.5 Listen again. After the beep, say the answer and listen to check your pronunciation.

7 🅐 **Make it personal** What are your plans for next week? Write at least five plans.

8.4 Is technology making us more, or less, social?

1 Replace the underlined mistakes in a–g with these words.

| answer | arguments | intends | ~~now~~ |
| sensitive | take | take place |

a I used to work in a restaurant but <u>actually</u> I work in an office. *(now)*
b When I was young my parents used to fight and have really angry <u>discussions</u>. It was terrible.
c Your cell phone is ringing, please <u>attend</u> it outside.
d The Coldplay concert will <u>realize</u> next weekend.
e People who do extreme sports <u>assume</u> a lot of risks.
f My smartphone screen is <u>sensible</u> to touch.
g My brother <u>pretends</u> to be a lawyer when he is older.

2 Now use the correct form of the underlined words from 1 to complete these sentences.

a I saw a great documentary the other day. Two scientists were having an interesting <u>discussion</u> about the future of technology.
b I don't know if she is at home but I _____ she is because the lights of her house are on.
c He has a good job but he isn't very _____ with his money. He always spends it on stupid things.
d Julia _____ that she couldn't move her leg so she didn't have to go to school.
e I was walking to the bus stop when I suddenly _____ that I forgot to lock my front door.
f Is Benicio Del Toro Mexican? I think he's Puerto Rican, _____.
g If you don't _____ all of your classes you will probably get a bad grade.

3 Read Valerie's vacation plans, then complete her email with the verb in the *simple present*, *present continuous* or *going to*.

4 ▶ 8.6 Look at the photos and choose the best form. Listen to check and repeat after the beep.

5 🎤 **Make it personal** Use the *simple present*, *present continuous*, *going to* or *will* to make four questions. Email them to a friend and share answers.

a What time / your next lesson / start / ?
_____
b What / you do / this weekend / ?
_____
c Do you think we / stop driving cars in the future / ?
_____
d You / do any homework tomorrow / ?
_____

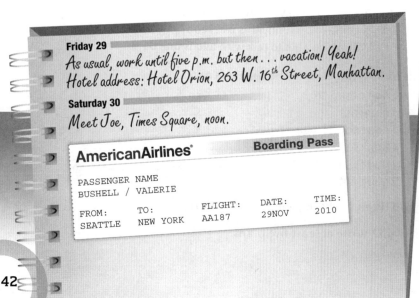

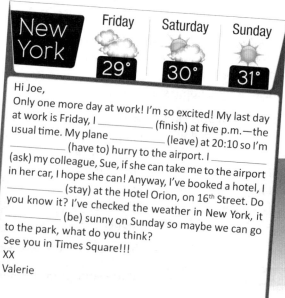

Hi Joe,
Only one more day at work! I'm so excited! My last day at work is Friday, I _____ (finish) at five p.m.—the usual time. My plane _____ (leave) at 20:10 so I'm _____ (have to) hurry to the airport. I _____ (ask) my colleague, Sue, if she can take me to the airport in her car, I hope she can! Anyway, I've booked a hotel, I _____ (stay) at the Hotel Orion, on 16th Street. Do you know it? I've checked the weather in New York, it _____ (be) sunny on Sunday so maybe we can go to the park, what do you think?
See you in Times Square!!!
XX
Valerie

42

8.5 Who do you talk to when you need help?

1 ▶8.7 Listen to these words and cross out the ones where the **bold** letter has a different sound.
   a ma**j**or   intelli**g**ent   **g**ive   langua**g**e
   b **h**ouse   **h**our   **h**eart   **h**otel
   c b**u**s   s**u**n   b**u**sy   s**o**mething

2 Reduce the Internet ads a–c to ten words each.

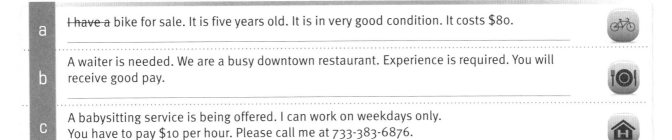

a	~~I have a~~ bike for sale. It is five years old. It is in very good condition. It costs $80.
b	A waiter is needed. We are a busy downtown restaurant. Experience is required. You will receive good pay.
c	A babysitting service is being offered. I can work on weekdays only. You have to pay $10 per hour. Please call me at 733-383-6876.

3 Read the horoscopes, then circle predictions *a*, *b* or *c* in 1–4.

Leo (Jul. 23 – Aug. 23)
You are sometimes a little aggressive and this can cause problems for you. If you argue too much, your colleagues won't want to talk with you. Try to pause before you speak and you will be OK.

Virgo (Aug. 24 – Sep. 22)
You have had a very busy life recently so now you need to relax. You will feel a lot better if you go on a short vacation. You'll probably spend more than usual but you will enjoy it. Worry about your bank account next month!

Libra (Sep. 23 – Oct. 23)
You'll feel very romantic this month. If you're in a relationship, your partner will be very surprised. If you're single, there's a good chance you'll meet someone new, so get out and have fun!

Scorpio (Oct. 24 – Nov. 21)
You will get some great career opportunities, but because of this you won't have much free time. Don't forget the important people in your life. If you give some time to them they will probably be able to help you.

1 Hi, I'm a Libra. Could you tell me if I'll meet a new boyfriend this month? Thanks.
   a) Definitely.   b) There's a good chance.   c) I doubt it.

2 Hi. I'm a Virgo, and I want to know if I will be rich this month.
   a) For sure.   b) Probably.   c) I doubt it.

3 Help! I had a lot of problems at work last month. Will this month be the same? By the way, I'm a Leo.
   a) Absolutely.   b) Perhaps.   c) Definitely not.

4 Hello. I'm a Scorpio, and I need to know if I'll be very busy this month.
   a) Definitely.   b) Maybe.   c) I doubt it.

4 ▶8.8 *Fortune-Teller!* Now listen to people 1–4 from 3, respond after the beep and check your pronunciation.

Connect
Look up your horoscope for today or this week online.

5 ▶8.9 **Make it personal** Match questions a–e to the answers. Listen to check and share your own answers with a friend.
   a Do you have a dishwasher?
   b Do you have a new phone?
   c Do you think 3D TV will be common?
   d Do you have any appointments this week?
   e Do you ever read your horoscope?

   ☐ I don't think so. I don't think people would like it.
   ☐ No I don't, but I wish I did. I hate doing the dishes.
   ☐ Only sometimes, for a laugh.
   ☐ Yes, I'm going to the dentist on Thursday.
   ☐ No, I've had this one for about a year now.

Can you remember …
➤ 6 appliances and devices? SB→p. 99
➤ how to use *-ing* to describe machines? SB→p. 99
➤ 7 technology phrasal verbs? SB→p. 100
➤ 5 adverbs to modify *will*? SB→p. 102
➤ the opposite of *I hope so*? SB→p. 103
➤ 5 false friends? SB→p. 104
➤ 4 verb forms to talk about the future? SB→p. 105
➤ 4 words for *fifty-fifty*? SB→p. 107

9 9.1 What do you think of marriage?

1 **Complete the puzzle with wedding words. Each symbol represents a letter.**

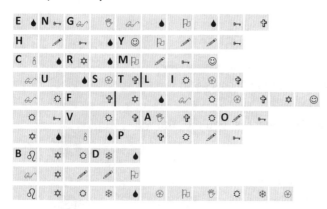

2 ▶9.1 **Match a–e to 1–5 to make funny quotes about marriage. Listen to check.**
   a Marriage is like a phone call in the night.
   b Marriage is a wonderful invention,
   c The secret of a happy marriage
   d Men marry women and hope they won't change.
   e My wife and I were happy for 20 years.
   1 remains a secret.
   2 First the ring, and then you wake up.
   3 Women marry men and hope that they will.
   4 Then we met.
   5 but then again, so is the bicycle repair kit.

3 **Complete a–e with *get* + one of these adjectives.**

   better   dark   dressed   lost   wet

   a What time does it _____ in the evening in winter?
   b I use the GPS on my smartphone so I don't _____.
   c Take two of these a day and you will _____ quickly.
   d You can stand under my umbrella so you don't _____.
   e In the mornings, I take a shower and then I _____.

4 **Read the article. Are a–g True (T), False (F) or Not mentioned (N)?**

   ## Wedding Traditions Around the World

   ### China
   In China today, it's common for the bride to wear several dresses on her wedding day. At the beginning of the wedding banquet the bride wears a traditional Chinese dress. This dress is red because that's a lucky color in China. In the middle of the banquet, she leaves and changes into a white Western-style wedding dress. After the banquet the bride will change into the final dress, a cocktail dress in her favorite color.

   ### Peru
   Peruvian weddings have a nice tradition involving the cake. Small gifts are put inside the wedding cake and attached to ribbons. Each unmarried female guest pulls a ribbon and one lucky woman will find a wedding ring. She will be the next bride.

   ### South Africa
   Zulu weddings are often very vibrant events. There are dance competitions between the bride and groom's families that symbolize the traditional antagonism between them. In very traditional weddings, the groom has to pay the bride's father before they can get married.

   ### UK
   An old tradition in the UK is that brides wear "something old" to symbolize continuity with the bride's family, "something new" to symbolize optimism for the future, "something borrowed" to symbolize good fortune, and "something blue" because that color was traditionally connected with love.

   a Chinese brides often wear four dresses in a day.
   b The dresses are usually different colors and styles.
   c In Peru, all of the single females receive a ring.
   d The guests have to eat the cake to find the gifts.
   e In South Africa, the best dancer gets a cake.
   f Zulu brides usually have to pay the groom's family.
   g In the UK, blue is traditionally a romantic color.

5 **Celebrity Marriage!** Order the words in a–c to make sentences. Complete them with a preposition + one of the names from the photos.
   a got / 2012 / Jessica Biel / to / married / _____ / _____ / .
   b Mark Zuckerberg / their garden / _____ / married / _____ / .
   c got / Michael Bublé / _____ / Luisana Lopilato / to / married / _____ / and Buenos Aires / .

Justin Timberlake

Vancouver

Priscilla Chan

6 **Make it personal** Which of the wedding traditions in 4 do you like best? Why?

44

9.2 Do you think romantic movies are entertaining?

1 Read Jen's diary and circle the correct adjective.

● *Sep. 13*
What a day! I was sitting in Mr. Stanton's science class, feeling **bored / boring** as usual. I was also **tired / tiring** because I'd been up late studying for an exam the night before. Then a new boy, Connor, came into the classroom and sat down next to me. He looks **amazed / amazing**, really good-looking. Anyway we talked and he's really **fun / funny** too, he made me laugh a lot. After class we sat together in the canteen and talked all the way through lunch time. I really like him!

● *Sep. 14*
The worst day ever! I had to do my presentation today, in front of about 400 people. I didn't know what to say and my stomach felt bad and my head felt dizzy. It was so **terrified / terrifying**! But then Viv did her presentation and I was really **surprised / surprising** 'coz it was really good. Usually she feels **scared / scary** in front of crowds of people but she said it was **excited / exciting**. Well done Viv!

● *Sep. 15*
Miss Innes said she was really **interested / interesting** in my presentation. I thought it was terrible but she said she was really **satisfied / satisfying** with it. Miss Innes said Viv's presentation was "**entertained**" / "**entertaining**". I don't know if that's good or bad!

2 Reread the article and circle the best option in a–d.
a Jen's writing about her **classes / school** in general.
b Mr. Stanton is a **teacher / the director**.
c Jen **likes / doesn't like** Mr. Stanton.
d Miss Innes **liked / didn't like** Jen's presentation.

3 ▶9.2 Listen to the sound effects. After the beep, say the full phrase with the best adjective.
a soccer match — boring / exciting / terrified
b she — bored / tiring / tired
c the result — surprised / surprising / excited
d he — scared / interesting / irritated
e the movie — terrifying / interested / bored

4 Complete the chart with adverbs. Which three mean the same?

Adjective	Adverb
absolute	absolutely
complete	
extreme	
real	
very	
total	

5 🙂 **Make it personal** Complete a–c with noun or gerund phrases and d–f with adjectives.
a For me, the most stressful day of the week is _____ because _____.
b The most exciting movie I've seen recently is _____.
c I'm really interested in _____.
d In my opinion, watching TV is _____.
e I usually feel _____ when I arrive at school.
f I feel _____ if I miss a bus or train.

6 ▶9.3 Listen and categorize the past tense forms of these verbs by number of syllables. Which two are irregular?

attract   break   cheat   date
dump   fall   flirt

1 syllable	2 syllables	3 syllables
lived	needed	remembered

7 ▶9.4 Listen and number the words from **6** in the order you hear them. Be careful! The verbs are not all in the same tense.

8 ▶9.4 Listen again. What do these numbers relate to? There's one extra number.

6   16   60   2003   2005

45

9.3 If you had three wishes, what would they be?

1 ▶9.5 Listen to a teacher at a job interview and complete the interviewer's questions.
   a What would you do if _____?
   b If your students _____, how would you control them?
   c _____ if there was a power outage?
   d _____, would you give yourself this job?

2 ▶9.6 Order the words in Mike's replies and match them to a–d in 1. Listen to check.
   a I / anything / wouldn't / do / .
   b I / of / yes / would / , / course / .
   c the / definitely / run / out / would / classroom / of / I / .
   d would / home / I / send / the / probably / students / .

3 🅐 Make it personal Write complete second conditional questions using the prompts in a–e.
   a you (be) the interviewer you (give) Mike the job?   *If you were...*
   b you (be) the teacher what you (do) next class?
   c you (can) travel anywhere where you (go)?
   d how you (feel) you (lose) your cell phone?
   e you (have) a million dollars what you (spend) it on?

4 ▶9.7 Match a–g to the cartoon pictures to make a joke. Listen to check.
   a The first man closed his eyes and said, "If I were in New York, I'd be the happiest man in the world."
   b They were very surprised when a genie appeared and gave them three wishes, one each.
   c "What's the matter?" asked the genie. "I'm so lonely," said the last man. "If my friends were here, I'd feel better."
   d "Poof!" The man disappeared. "Wow! That's amazing!" said the woman. She closed her eyes and said, "My wish is that… I were in Paris!"
   e There were three people stuck on a desert island in the middle of the Pacific Ocean. One day, they found a lamp on the beach, so they picked it up and rubbed it.
   f The genie immediately gave the man his wish and brought his friends back to the island.
   g "Poof!" The woman disappeared, and the last man immediately started crying.

5 ▶9.8 Match the **bold** letters in a–e to the sound pictures. Listen to check and repeat the sentences.
   a An interesting **g**eography **j**ournal.
   b He is a **j**ealous e**d**itor.
   c The i**d**ea of marria**g**e terrifies him.
   d The e**dg**e of my **d**iary is beautiful.
   e It's **g**enuinely **d**ifferent.

9.4 Have you ever performed for an audience?

1 ▶9.9 Mark the syllables and stress in these words, as in the example. Listen to check.

a ●•• actor
b athlete
c comedian
d guitarist
e gymnast
f celebrity
g runner
h magician

2 ▶9.10 Listen to a couple talking. What has the woman lost? Why does she say "I must be getting old"?

3 ▶9.10 Listen again and complete the chart.

Location that the man suggests	Reason	The woman agrees ✓ or disagrees ✗	Reason
living room			
	She often leaves her glasses there.		
			She doesn't need them for typing.
	They must be somewhere.	✓	

4 Match a–f to 1–6 in the second column to make deductions. Then match three of them to photos 1–3.

a You haven't eaten anything all day.
b Are you crazy? It's 35° C.
c Where's Angela today?
d I know Karen and Liz,
e You've been at school all day.
f That's absolutely ridiculous.

1 so you must be Ellie. Nice to finally meet you.
2 You must have learned something.
3 You must be really hungry.
4 You can't possibly be cold.
5 You can't be serious.
6 She might be sick. She didn't look very well yesterday.

5 ▶9.11 Cover the second column. Listen and, after the beep, make a deduction.

6 **Make it personal** Who is a successful person you admire? Why are they successful? Write a paragraph about the person.

Connect
Record your paragraph on your phone and send it to a classmate or your teacher.

9.5 How do you get on with your siblings?

1 Read the article. True (T), False (F) or Not mentioned (N)?
  a The twins have won over 50 singles titles each.
  b The boys are exactly the same height.
  c Their parents were worried about the way they communicated as children.
  d They shared winning when they were younger.
  e They watched a lot of tennis stars on TV when they were children.
  f The twins' charity builds schools in the U.S.

Tennis Twins

Americans Bob and Mike Bryan are the most successful tennis doubles team in history. The guys have won multiple Olympic medals, including Gold in 2012 and have won more games, matches, tournaments and grand slams than any other team. They have been the number one team eight times and have won at least five titles per year for ten years. A very impressive record! _____ are also identical twin brothers, although Bob is about three centimeters taller. So, has being a twin helped _____ be so successful?

Well, their communication on the tennis court is amazing and this goes back to _____ shared childhood. _____ finish each other's sentences and know what the other is thinking. When they were around six their parents took _____ to therapy because they were speaking an "alien twin language"! They are so close that they don't need to speak to communicate. It just comes naturally, and this makes _____ very dangerous to their opponents. _____ parents thought it was important that their children had fun playing tennis and they didn't want the boys to compete with each other. If _____ played each other in singles competitions, they would share victories. In one competition Bob would win, and Mike would win in the next. Of course, being able to practice with an expert player every day has helped _____ become so good at tennis.

But tennis isn't the only thing _____ are good at. They have played music since they were young and they recorded _____ first album in 2004. One thing they didn't have when they were young was TV. _____ dad took it out of the house so they had lots of time to practice music and tennis. And this could be the reason why they are so successful today! The guys do a lot of charity work too. Their organization, Bryan Bros. Foundation, helps children around the world to have a better quality of life.

2 ▶9.12 Reread the article and complete with *they*, *them* or *their*. Listen to check.

3 Insert the missing word in suggestions a–e.
  a Why you go to bed?
  b If I you, I'd call her.
  c should study more often.
  d What putting an ad on the Internet?
  e You better eat something.

4 ▶9.13 Listen to five problems and, after the beep, give some advice from 3. Listen to check.

Can you remember ...

▶ 10 wedding words? SB▶p. 112
▶ 5 relationship words? SB▶p. 114
▶ the difference between *bored* and *boring*? SB▶p. 115
▶ 6 adverbs to make adjectives sound stronger? SB▶p. 115
▶ 3 performers ending -*or*, -*er* and -*ian*? SB▶p. 118
▶ 4 modal verbs for making guesses? SB▶p. 118
▶ 5 ways to make suggestions? SB▶p. 121

10.1 Do you often feel stressed?

1 ▶10.1 Listen to a woman talking about stress and circle the correct word / phrase.
   a The woman is **stressed** / **an expert on stress** / **having stress therapy**.
   b She talks about **two** / **three** / **four** types of stress.
   c Acute stress is caused by **positive** / **negative** / **both positive and negative** experiences.
   d Chronic stress is **sometimes** / **often** / **always** bad for you.
   e She talks about the **financial** / **physical** / **emotional** effects of stress.

2 ▶10.1 Listen again and complete the brochure with one word in each gap.

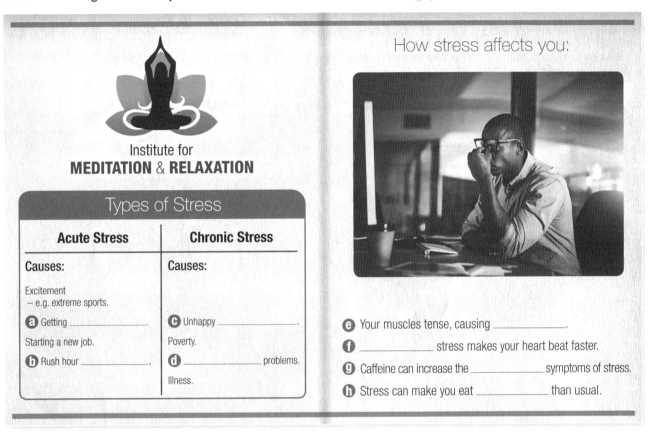

Connect
Look up ways to reduce stress online.

3 **Make it personal** Using the brochure, decide what kind of stress these stressors cause, acute (A) or chronic (C). Have you ever experienced any of these?
   a Financial problems.
   b Caring for a child every day.
   c A deadline at work or school.
   d Multitasking in the morning.
   e Lack of sleep for two months.

4 Use **over** or **under** + the verb in parentheses to complete these sentences.
   a These potatoes are _____ (**cook**). They are still hard.
   b Most soccer players have too much money. They are incredibly _____ (**pay**).
   c I always _____ (**eat**) at Christmas. There's so much delicious food!
   d I can't use my credit card anymore, I have _____ (**spend**) this month.
   e The coach _____ (**estimate**) the opposition team and didn't use his best players, so his team lost 4–1.

5 ▶10.2 Words beginning **s** + consonant can be difficult to pronounce. Listen and repeat these two groups. Don't put a vowel sound before the **s**.
   a stressed   start   sleep   snack
   b smoke   spend   spoiled school

 /s/

10.2 Would you like to change anything in your life

1 Study the chart and correct two mistakes in each of a–e.

✋ (completely stop)	− (change)	+ (change)
I want to quit my job. (noun)	I want to work less. (verb)	I want to exercise more. (verb)
I need to quit smoking. (verb + -ing)	I want to eat less salt. (verb + noun)	I want to get more sleep. (verb + noun)

   a That's a cough bad. Why don't you quit to smoke?
   b Ugh! Your cooking is so salty. You should to use salt less.
   c I'm not going lend you any money so you'd better spending less.
   d You don't play any sports and you drive everywhere. Why you don't exercising more?
   e You won't pass your school test if you don't study more and to watch TV less.

2 ▶10.3 Listen and respond to each statement after the beep using the advice in 1. Follow the model.
   Model: *Ugh! Your cooking is so salty!*   You: *You should use less salt.*

3 Complete the clues with **who** or **that**. Match six of them to photos a–f and do the crossword.

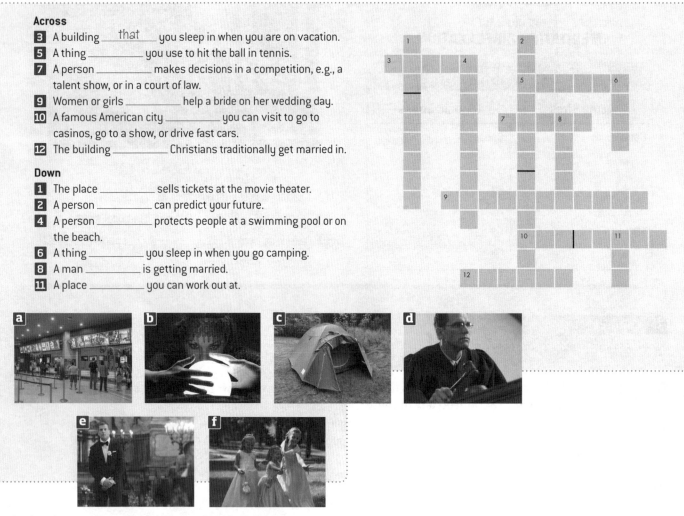

Across
3 A building ___that___ you sleep in when you are on vacation.
5 A thing _____ you use to hit the ball in tennis.
7 A person _____ makes decisions in a competition, e.g., a talent show, or in a court of law.
9 Women or girls _____ help a bride on her wedding day.
10 A famous American city _____ you can visit to go to casinos, go to a show, or drive fast cars.
12 The building _____ Christians traditionally get married in.

Down
1 The place _____ sells tickets at the movie theater.
2 A person _____ can predict your future.
4 A person _____ protects people at a swimming pool or on the beach.
6 A thing _____ you sleep in when you go camping.
8 A man _____ is getting married.
11 A place _____ you can work out at.

4 Order the words in a–c to make descriptions.
   a place / books / that / lends / a / .
   b clean / that / a / use / house / you / your / to / thing / .
   c new / who / constructs / person / a / houses / .

5 ▶10.4 Listen to check and write down the name of the person, place, or object.

6 🎤 **Make it personal** Think of three things you'd like to change in your life. Why do you want to change them? How would you change them? Record your answers.

50

10.3 What's your attitude to money?

1 Read the article and put the paragraphs a–c in the correct order. Then complete paragraph *a* with the correct form of these verbs. There's one extra word.

afford   cost   earn   pay for   spend   win

From the Streets to Success

a Topitop is successful because it constantly produces new styles at prices customers can _____. For example, a surf shirt from Topitop _____ approximately US$10, half the price of an imported equivalent. Middle-class Peruvians, families that _____ on average US$550 a month, can _____ their money at Topitop and still have enough money to _____ a movie ticket.

b Aquilino Flores was born in poverty, high up in the Andes mountains. He was 12 when he left home and traveled to Lima, the capital of Peru, to work, and his first job there was washing cars. He earned just enough money to live and nothing more, but Aquilino was a good worker and a friendly guy, and one day one of his customers suggested that he sell T-shirts. The man gave Aquilino 20 T-shirts and he sold them in one day. That is how Aquilino Flores started in the fashion industry.

c Now his company, Topitop, is the largest clothes producer in Peru and makes over US$275 million a year. The company has stores all over Peru, as well as Venezuela, and also exports clothes to Brazil, Europe and the U.S., where the clothes are sold as Hugo Boss, North Face and other famous and expensive brand names.

2 Read the website and match the titles to a–e.

Bargain   Earn Money   Lend Your Money
Save Your Money   Win Money

Top Ways to Get Rich

a _____
The traditional way to make money is to get a job and spend all day working. This has its disadvantages. It can be…
click to read more

b _____
The lottery is a good way to make a lot of money very quickly. All you have to do is buy a ticket and hope. Of course, you will… *click to read more*

c _____
Don't pay more for things than you have to. Before you go shopping, find out how much different items cost in different places and on the Internet. NEVER spend more than you can afford and don't be scared to ask for a discount. Although this can be… *click to read more*

d _____
When you get some money, don't spend it—it's that simple. Some bank accounts will even pay you a percentage to leave your money in the bank. Of course, it will be…
click to read more

e _____
If the banks can do it, why can't you? Let people borrow money from you and then make them pay a large percentage on what they borrow. This can be…
click to read more

3 ▶10.5 **Make it personal** Listen to check and find one disadvantage to each suggestion. Which suggestion is the best for you?

4 Read the extracts from the freeganism video on p. 129 of the Student's Book. Then replace the underlined slang words with their synonyms.

carry   abandoned   excited   house
pick it up   take   those things

"I live in New York City, where I think it's pretty common to pick up <u>trashed</u> furniture or electronics, because people here just leave <u>that stuff</u> on the sidewalk for you to <u>grab</u>. And when you're on your way home and you walk by a perfectly good piece of furniture that you can use, why not just <u>scoop it up</u> and <u>schlep</u> it back to your <u>abode</u>?"

"I'm <u>psyched</u>!"

10.4 How often do you post on social media?

1 Read the text about Bruno Mars and order the words in a–f to make questions.

24k Magic!

Bruno Mars has been a performer for _____ years. He has had _____ number-one singles and he's won nearly _____ awards, including eleven Grammys and four Guinness World Records. Amazingly, over _____ people watched Bruno perform at Morumbi Stadium in São Paulo in _____ . That concert alone made over $ _____ !

a long / singer / been / has / a / how / Bruno / ?
b singles / how / had / he / number-one / has / many / ?
c he / awards / many / has / won / how / ?
d São Paulo / many / how / people / him / watched / in / ?
e in / when / he / São Paulo / perform / did / ?
f how / money / make / did / concert / the / much?

2 ▶10.6 Listen to an interview to check the questions and complete Bruno's biography.

> 🔊 **Connect**
> *Go online and find information about a musician or band you like.*

3 Use the prompts to write questions about units 6–9. Do the quiz and look back to check.

ID QUIZ

1 **Where / Laura / want / go for her 30ᵗʰ birthday / ?** *Where did Laura want to go for her 30ᵗʰ birthday?*
   a) Jamaica b) Las Vegas c) Barcelona

2 **What event / Charlie / do / ?** _____
   a) marathon b) triathlon c) heptathlon

3 **Which soccer team / Jason / love?** _____
   a) Liverpool b) Tottenham c) Manchester United

4 **What / Barbara / collect / ?** _____
   a) traffic cones b) miniature chairs c) toys

5 **How many jobs / lose / because of illegal downloads / ?** _____
   a) around 500 b) about 50,000 c) over 70,000

6 **What music / the guy / request in lesson 8.1 / ?** _____
   a) Mozart b) Justin Bieber c) Britney Spears

7 **According to Penny Duff, how / we / communicate in / future / ?** _____
   a) telepathy b) email c) with lasers

8 **What / Matt Jones / offer help with?** _____
   a) finances b) careers c) health and diet

9 **How high / be / a "Marriage in the Sky" / ?** _____
   a) 30 meters b) 40 meters c) 50 meters

10 **How many / countries / they / operate in / ?** _____
   a) 30 b) 40 c) 50

4 ▶10.7 Listen to the sound pictures and put these words in the correct column according to the sound of the **bold** letters.

consump**tio**n   conven**tio**nal   deci**si**on   lei**su**re   occa**si**on   participa**tio**n

1 /ʃ/	**2** /ʒ/

5 ▶10.8 Listen to check and repeat the words.

10.5 Do you enjoy reading in English?

1 Read the story and, as you read, answer 1–5.

Class of '99

The taxi drove downtown and Nick looked at the low gray building. Has it really been twenty years since he was last here? Through the double doors, everything was exactly as he remembered it, although a little smaller now, and strangely quieter. The Principal's office was on the right, next to the nurse's room. He turned left and followed the signs: "Class of '99 Reunion."

1 What is the low gray building?

He found the gym and waited in the doorway watching the middle-aged people standing in uncomfortable groups of 4, 5 or 6. Who did he remember? That tall man holding two glasses of orange cocktail in his big hands, and drinking from both, must be Jed, the football star. The girls loved him, almost as much as he loved himself.

2 Why should Nick remember the middle-aged people?

Nick picked up a glass of orange cocktail from the table and walked slowly around the room, trying hard to remember faces. The cocktail had a sour, toxic taste. "Nick, is that you?" said a quiet voice. Turning, he saw a small man in an expensive suit, his blue eyes behind thick glasses. Marcus! Nick smiled, happy to see a face that he knew and happy also that the quiet, shy, hardworking kid was now apparently a successful adult.

3 Why does Nick think that Marcus is successful?

"Isn't that cocktail awful? Try this," said Marcus as he replaced Nick's glass. Nick took the beer and the two started talking. Nick was divorced and working in a hotel, Marcus was unmarried and working for a pharmaceutical company.
Suddenly a loud voice: "Well, little mouse Marcus... squeak, squeak!" and a massive hand hit Marcus in the back. For a second, Marcus's face showed terror, then anger, before returning to calm.

4 Who do you think hit Marcus?

"Jed?" said Marcus. Suddenly Nick remembered the horrible names, the broken glasses, the physical and mental torture that was Marcus's life and Jed's amusement for four years of adolescent prison. "Of course it is. I'll be back to talk with you later, Mouse." said Jed, pressing Marcus's glasses with his finger. As Jed walked away laughing, Marcus watched him, his eyes burning with anger.

5 How does Marcus feel about Jed?

"Nick, I have to go now," said Marcus. "You were always so kind to me, but I don't think we'll meet again." He paused and then added "And Nick, don't drink any more of that cocktail."

6 What do you think Marcus did to Jed's cocktail?

2 This story is approximately 400 words long. Try to reread it in two minutes.

3 These workbook texts are approximately 200 words long each. Time yourself and see how fast you can read them. Then try again another day and see if you are faster.

Text and lesson	Target time	1st reading	2nd reading	3rd reading	4th reading
A Success Story (7.4)	60 seconds				
Horoscopes (8.5)	75 seconds				
Wedding Traditions (9.1)	75 seconds				

4 ▶10.9 Add *one* or *ones* in three places in each dialogue. Listen to check.

a **Customer** I'd like to buy some shoes.

Salesperson Of course. Which would you like to try?

Customer I like the black in the window.

Salesperson Certainly. What size are you?

Customer I'm a 13.

Salesperson Ah. I'm afraid we don't have size 13, but our other store might have them. The next to the movie theater.

b **Customer** I'm making a fruit salad. Do you have any grapes?

Salesperson Yes, we have purple and green. Which would you like?

c **Customer** Do you have any guidebooks for the city?

Salesperson Yes. This has a good map and this has lots of historical information.

Customer I'll take the with the map, please.

Can you remember ...

➤ 9 common causes of stress? SB→p.124

➤ 12 suggestions for relieving stress? SB→p.125

➤ 2 relative pronouns? SB→p.127

➤ 8 money verbs? SB→p.128

➤ 3 adverbs that can go after *how* in a question? SB→p.130

53

Audioscript

Unit 1

▶ 1.5

C = Chris   R = Rachel

C Ah! That's the pizza, I'll get it. Uh, Rachel, I don't have enough money. Can I borrow some?

R I don't have any with me. What about that money Andy gave you?

C Oh, yes, that's right. I'll go and get it.

R OK. Let's eat! Is this the vegetarian? Chris it's enormous. I won't eat all that.

C Don't worry, I can help.

R Well thanks for the offer, but I think I'll take it home with me.

▶ 1.6

1 Will you buy any clothes this weekend?

2 What time will you get up tomorrow?

3 What will you do after you finish your homework?

4 Will you go to the countryside soon?

5 What will you eat for dinner?

▶ 1.9

B = boy   W = woman   M = man

1 B Mom... MOM!

W What is it?

B What's going on? It's Saturday morning.

W Oh, your grandparents just called. They're coming for a surprise visit and, well, you know what grandma's like. She likes everything just perfect...

B Oh, right. Do you want some help?

W Oh, yes, please, love. Can you wash the dishes for me? And...

2 M Mmmmmm. What's that smell? It smells delicious.

W Oh, I'm making seafood lasagna.

M Ah! My favorite dish. You're fantastic. Do you want me to help?

W Uhm. You can make me a cup of coffee if you want.

3 M What are you doing?

W I'm fixing my bike.

M Can I help you?

W Ummm. Can you pass me that Allen key, please? No, not that. The Allen key. It looks like a big "L".

M Sure. Here you are.

W Thank you.

Unit 2

▶ 2.1

Uh, I only buy one newspaper a week on Sundays. Uh, it's really big and has a lot of supplements, so it takes me an entire week to read it all! Of course, they always put the most important news on the front page, and they, uh, they often give the newspaper's opinion about it in an article, I think that's usually very interesting. Umm, they have all the soccer results in a separate section, in the sports section, and I usually read that on the weekend. Uh, what else? Oh, they also have a TV guide in a magazine, so you know what's on TV. I read that during the week. To be honest, the rest of the magazine is often a waste of paper. If an important piece of news happens during the week, I just read about it on the Internet, uh, you know, on my tablet.

▶ 2.2

A How often do you buy a newspaper?

B How often do you use a social media site?

C Do you listen to the news on the radio?

D Are you interested in celebrity gossip?

E Did you watch the news on TV yesterday?

▶ 2.5

a Scandal in the news today as a powerful businessman is accused of paying over two hundred thousand dollars to politicians as part of a development scheme. Here's our business reporter, Kimberley Chu, with more details.

b Over 200 million gallons of oil entered the Gulf of Mexico. This is possibly the world's worst environmental contamination disaster.

c ... announced today that there will be a new government initiative to end the financial problems of millions across the country. Great news for families that live on less than $5 a day. They will finally receive real government support. That means...

d The police apprehended the leader of a drug-trafficking gang in his home last night. Reports say that they found over $50,000 inside a refrigerator as well as a collection of 13 assault rifles. Francisco Giannini, known as "the pirate," was arrested...

e Scientists claim that there is a major downward tendency in the volume of polar sea ice. They can prove a reduction of 70% over the last 30 years during the summer months.

f The number of young people, aged 16-25, without jobs is rising, says a new government report. Figures show numbers are up from 2.5 million last year to 2.8 million.

g A century ago, there were around 100,000 tigers. Today, after losing almost 93% of their territory, there are only approximately 3,200 animals.

h The number of influenza vaccinations for people over 65 is growing worldwide. In 2011, Mexico had the highest rate of vaccination, at 88.2%, followed by Chile at 87.9%.

▶ 2.7

1 What's your favorite kind of weather?

2 What's the weather like right now?

3 Does it rain a lot in your city?

4 Do you ever have floods or droughts?

5 Do you have earthquakes in your country?

▶ 2.8

1 H = Hannah   A = Abby

A Hannah, Hannah! Guess what! I saw Meghan Markle today!

H Abby! You didn't! What happened?

A Well, I was working with some kids when suddenly the door opened and and she walked into the library with Prince Harry. It was crazy! I didn't know what to do.

H No! You're joking! I'm sure the kids loved her.

2 M = man   P = Pete

M Pete, what happened to your car?

P I don't know. I was watching TV when I heard this loud BANG! So I went outside and found my car like this.

M Oh dear. That's really bad luck. How much will it cost to repair?

3 M = man   Z = Zoe

M Hey, Zoe. Congratulations on your new job. How did you get it?

Z Oh, I was really lucky. I was talking to these people on the bus about my college course and they offered me a job in their laboratory. I couldn't believe it!

M Wow, that is lucky. Can you ask them to give me a job too?

▶ 2.11

W = woman   M = man

1 W1 I was shopping on Saturday. I had a lot of beautiful clothes, but then, for some reason, my credit card didn't work. The stupid machine couldn't read it!

W2 Oh dear. That's bad luck.

2 M1 While I was walking in the park I found twenty dollars.

W3 Wow! That's lucky.

54

Audioscript

3 W4 I decided not to go to school on Tuesday, I went to the city with my friends. We were sitting in a café and my dad saw me.

W5 Oh, dear. That's bad luck.

4 M2 There was a storm when I was walking home yesterday, but suddenly my mom drove past and she picked me up in the car.

W6 Wow! That's lucky.

5 M3 I was visiting the zoo on the weekend and I saw a chimpanzee take a tourist's camera. And then, get this, the chimpanzee took a photo. I couldn't believe it!

W7 No! You're joking.

6 M4 I was with my friends the other day. We were playing soccer in the park and guess what! Some Barcelona players came and joined us. It was unbelievable.

M5 No! You're joking.

▶ 2.12

M = man   W = woman

M This crazy thing happened to me at work the other day.

W Oh, yeah? What happened?

M Well, we got this call to go to a house because a woman was on fire.

W What! Why was she on fire?

M Apparently, she had some stones that caught fire in her pocket.

W Wait a minute? The stones caught fire?

M Yeah, they had some kind of chemical that reacts with oxygen.

W No way! So, is she OK?

M Yeah, the paramedics took her to the hospital but she had some severe burns.

Unit 3

▶ 3.2

J = Jed   T = Tanya

J Hi... excuse me... hi. I'm doing a survey about online shopping. Do you have a minute?

T Uh, yeah, I guess.

J Great! Uh... I'm Jed. What's your name?

T Uh... I'm Tanya.

J Oh, that's great! Now, let's get started Tanya. Uh... could you look at this list of products and tell me: what have you bought this month; what have you bought in the last six months; and what have you never bought online.

T Sure, that sounds easy! Well, let's see. Uh, books, yeah I buy a lot of books online. I'm a student and it's a lot cheaper to get the things I need from a website, and, uh,

many bookstores don't sell them—they are kind of specific. Umm, music. Sure, I download a lot of songs from the Internet, uh, legally, of course! And sometimes movies too. I watched a great one last weekend, and the weekend before, so yeah, twice this month.

J OK, and how about vacations? Have you ever booked a vacation online? You know, travel tickets, hotel rooms. That kind of thing.

T Uh, travel tickets and hotel rooms. Well, I don't have much money and, uh, vacations are kind of expensive. I've never booked a vacation online, I, uh, I usually go and stay with some friends near the ocean and they drive so I don't need to book anything! Event tickets, well, I went to see a concert a couple of months ago and I booked that online, it was really easy. Uh, next is "electronic equipment". You mean like cameras and MP3 players and things like that, right?

J Uh-huh.

T Well, no, I've never bought any of that kind of stuff online. I don't trust the delivery service with expensive equipment, and, well, what if they drop it or something? No, I don't think so. And finally, clothes. Well this T-shirt came from an online store, but my boyfriend bought it for me. I've never actually bought clothes online, I want to try them on first, you know? In fact, I went shopping for shoes today.

J Yeah, a lot of people say that. Well thank you very much and have a nice day.

T You too.

▶ 3.4

M = man   W = woman   B = boy

M Honey, it's almost 7:30. Are you ready to go?

W We can't go now. The dogsitter hasn't arrived yet.

M The what?

W You know, that boy from down the road. He's going to look after the dog while we're away.

M Oh right. I forgot about the dog! He's late again. OK. I'll give him a call.

W I can't find my glasses. Hon, have you seen my glasses?

M I've already told you. They're in the living room, on the laptop.

W Ah! Honey, the dogsitter's here.

B Hi Mr. Adams, how are you?

M Hi. Good, thanks. Come in, come in.

W Have you fed the dog yet, George?

M No, I haven't. Just a minute.

B Hi Mrs. Adams. You look nice.

W Oh, thanks dear. Now I've put her food and toys and everything in this bag.

B Oh, I've already bought some food for her.

W Oh, really? That was very nice of you. All ready? Let's go.

B Bye, see you next week.

M/W See you.

M Oh no! I've just remembered!

W What is it hon?

M I've left our passports at home. I'm such an idiot!

W Oh, George! Not again! You...

▶ 3.7

M = man   W = woman

B = boy   G = girl

1 M1 My dog can speak French.

W1 Wait a minute. Did I hear you say that your dog can speak French?

2 W2 The Internet is a complete waste of time.

M2 I'm sorry, I don't agree. I think it's a part of life now.

3 M3 I'm sorry to have to tell you that Santa Claus doesn't exist.

B1 What do you mean he doesn't exist?

4 B2 I can play the guitar with my teeth.

G1 Really, you never told me you could do that before.

Unit 4

▶ 4.1

Typical blood type A jobs are software engineer or librarian, jobs that suit their quiet personality. Type B people are creative so they are often cooks, hairstylists or journalists. Type ABs are a strange group, they could be anything, but they are often lawyers or teachers. They are also very romantic and can match any other blood type. Finally the type Os. These people are often top athletes, bank managers or politicians.

▶ 4.2

When I was young I used to love being in the kitchen with my mom.

One day I was helping her to make a cake. We put it in the oven and then... we heard these really strange noises. Something was making a small "beep... beep... beep". We looked in the kitchen but we couldn't find it, so we emptied all the cupboards. Nothing.

So we went into the living room and looked under the sofa, behind the TV, everywhere. Still nothing.

55

Audioscript

So we went into the garage and looked in all the boxes and all the cupboards. And then we found it.

It was an old smoke alarm and the battery was dying: "beep...beep...beep".

We went back into the kitchen and guess what! It was full of smoke! The cake was burning!

▶ 4.7

S = salesperson   C = customer

S Hello, can I help you?

C Yes, I'm looking for a gift for my nephew's birthday.

S OK, well, how old is your nephew?

C He's going to be 21.

S Oh, well, that is an important birthday. You should definitely get him something special.

C Yes, but I really don't know what to get him. Could you give me some ideas?

S Sure, uhmm well, have you considered buying him some new technology? This is the new *Eye-let Mini* tablet, it's really popular with young people and...

C Hmm, I think he already has a tablet. And I was hoping to buy something a little cheaper than two hundred and ninety-nine dollars. Maybe around twenty dollars.

S Twenty dollars? Have you thought about getting him a nice book? We have a very big selection of...

C Oh, no, no. He doesn't like reading. Well, not books anyway! And I want to get him something more... uh, more appealing for his age.

S Hmmm, well I shouldn't say this madam, but 21-year-olds always need money. Why don't you give him some money so he can buy what he wants?

C Yes, that's a good idea. Thank you.

Unit 5

▶ 5.1

1 Hi, I'm Vicki. Um, uh, I always wanted to defend clients in court, like in the movies, but now I work for a business in the city. I check all the legal documents—contracts, that kind of thing.

2 Hello, I'm Ben and I work in a pharmaceutical laboratory outside the city. I couldn't do this job without my degree.

3 Hi, my name's Kathy and I run a small company right here in California. My degree helped me to understand marketing, management and economics.

4 Hi, I'm Ross. Uh... well I work for the government planning bridges and roads,

all the major construction that happens around here.

5 My name's Rose and I work with business people from the U.S. or Canada, and even China sometimes. I help them with conferences and meetings. And I translate documents too.

▶ 5.2

1 Hi, my name is Helen and I study at Brinton College. I chose this college because it's a long way from home and it's good because it has an attractive campus. I'm studying for a bachelor's in business and I really like it because of the good teachers. One day, I want to make a million dollars—a month!

2 Hi, my name is Janet and I study at Arleston College. I chose this college because I can get here easily and it's good because it has babysitting facilities. I'm studying for a vocational certificate in cooking and I really like it because of the evening classes. One day, I want to open a café.

▶ 5.3

OK, so here are the answers. Officially you can't drive a dirty car in Russia, although many people do of course. In most countries you can only get married without permission from your parents at 18. However, in other countries, including Bolivia, Paraguay and Peru, you don't have to have permission to get married at 16. In some countries it is even younger. Chewing gum and bubble gum are both illegal in Singapore, you can't buy it anywhere. Strange, huh? There are some strange licenses around the world. For example, you have to have a license to own a dog in Canada and you can't have a TV without a license in the UK. On the other hand, you don't have to carry any personal ID in the UK or in the U.S. In many countries around the world it is compulsory to participate in elections. Until recently, this was true in Chile and Venezuela but now voting is voluntary. There citizens do not have to vote. Brazil still has military service for its citizens. All men have to register when they are 18, and women can choose to register as well, if they want to.

▶ 5.5

Hello and welcome to Streetwise College. I hope you are going to enjoy your time here and, before we give you a tour of the facilities, I would like to offer you some advice to help you make the most of your time here. First, your education is your responsibility, so be enthusiastic about what you are learning. When you are really into a topic it's a lot easier to learn. If you want to optimize your classes, you

can download material about the topic in advance. You will benefit a lot more if you already understand a little about the topic of each lesson. Now this next piece of advice depends on your course, but, in most cases, you will have to do a lot of reading, so find a good online dictionary so you can look up new academic words and then use them when you write a paper. The next point is very important: don't miss too many classes! If you are absent from too many classes, we will ask you to leave the college. Now, as you will see, this is a big campus but you can use the college portal to find out exactly where your classes are and what time they start, and you can store the info on your phone planner. And finally, I know that at times you will be under a lot of pressure. If you find that the school work is too much for you, don't drop out. Of course, college can be difficult, but talk to your teacher, we are here to help. Any questions? OK, and now we will show you around the campus...

▶ 5.7

M = man   W = woman

M Uhm... honey. I'm not getting out of bed today.

W What?

M If I do, you'll divorce me.

W Oh no, not again! Get up Dan.

M Look. If I get up, I'll go to work.

W And?

M Well, when I go to work, I'll meet my friends.

W Yeah?

M And, see, if I meet my friends, we'll go out.

W Hmmm.

M And if we go out, you'll get jealous.

W But...

M And if you get jealous, you'll divorce me. So, I'm staying in bed.

W And I... am leaving. Goodbye!

Unit 6

▶ 6.7

I = interviewer

I Today we are asking tourists on the streets of Madrid what they think about Spain's famous bull-running.

1 S Hi, Shane here. I love running with the bulls, it's a real adrenaline rush, you know? I go every year if I can. Last year I actually touched a bull on the head. It was so cool!

2 P Hi there. I'm Petra, from New Orleans. I've seen the bull running on TV and

56

Audioscript

there's no way I would ever do that. Not in a million years! I think it's really stupid and the bulls are obviously tormented by all the people around them. Poor animals!

3 J Hi, I'm Jake, from St. Louis, in the U.S. Yeah, I'd love to run with the bulls. It looks really crazy. I used to play college football, so I think I would be good at it.

4 L I'm Lucia. Hmmm, I guess I'd like to try it. Maybe just once though. And I would want to practice running in a crowded place first, maybe in a metro station or somewhere like that.

▶ 6.8

M = man   W = woman

a M1 I'm bored with this program, aren't you?

W1 It's OK, but I've seen it before. I'll turn it off.

M1 So, what do you want to do this evening?

W1 Hmm, I don't know. Do you want to go to the movies? Or, there's a band playing.

M1 I don't feel like watching a movie. Let's go and see the band.

b W2 Would you like a drink?

M2 It's OK, I'll get it. Would you like a beer?

W2 No, thanks. I'm on an alcohol-free diet.

M2 Oh. So, how about a Coke?

W2 Uh, I'd rather have an orange juice, please.

M2 OK. One orange juice coming up.

▶ 6.9

M = man   W = woman

W1 So, what did you think of the band?

M1 Uh... well... they were OK, I guess.

W1 You mean you didn't like them?

M1 Well, uh... they were kind of loud and I prefer listening to quieter bands.

W1 Oh. Well, I thought they were great. I'd love to see them again!

Unit 7

▶ 7.4

M = man   W = woman

a M Do you collect anything?

W Yeah, I have a collection of coffee cups.

M How many do you have?

W About 50.

b W Are you into sports?

M Yeah, I love tennis.

W How often do you play?

M About once a week.

c M Do you have a favorite artist?

W I'm really into Beyoncé.

M Have you ever seen her perform?

W Unfortunately, no, I haven't.

d W Which soccer team do you like?

M I'm a United fan.

W Have you ever been to a game?

M Yeah, I went last year.

▶ 7.9

J = Jess   H = Helen

J Hi Helen, how's it going?

H Hi Jess, yes, I'm good thanks. Hey, I was hoping you could do me a favor next week. I've got this interview and... uh Jess, are you OK? What's going on there?

J Oh, I'm just watching Big Brother. I don't know where they find these people, they are just so stupid, you know?

H What? Big Brother! That's a terrible show, they're just idiots. Anyway, uh, Jess. Could you...

J I mean, this man on here now is crying because he tried to cook something and it burned and the other people are screaming because there is smoke in the kitchen. They are all idiots! Anyway Helen, how can I help?

H So, as I was saying, I have this interview next week and I'm kind of, you know, kind of nervous. So I was hoping I could practice interviewing with you, you know, just so I feel more confident.

J Yeah, sure, no problem. Come whenever you want.

H Thanks Jess.

Unit 8

▶ 8.4

a Will 3D TV be common in five years?

b Will there be a World War 3?

c Did we have homework from the last class?

d Are we going to have a test this week?

e Is it going to be sunny this weekend?

f Will we be able to communicate with aliens one day?

Unit 9

▶ 9.2

M = man   W = woman

a M1 GOAL!!!

M2 The soccer match is exciting.

b W1 I'm going to bed, good night.

M2 She is tired.

c M3 That was the weather report and now the sports. The result of today's friendly match between France and Switzerland is... France 1 – Switzerland 5.

M2 The result is surprising.

d M4 Come on!

M2 He is irritated.

e W2 No, please no...

M2 The movie is terrifying.

▶ 9.4

Actor and model Ashton Kutcher met actress Demi Moore at a dinner party in New York in 2003, they were extremely attracted to each other and they talked all night. Many people were surprised because Demi is 16 years older than Ashton.

They fell in love and got married in 2005. Rumors started in the media that Ashton cheated on Demi almost immediately after the wedding.

Ashton's friends say that he was very loyal to Demi and never flirted with other women when he was with her.

However, after six years Demi decided to break up with Ashton. Why did she dump him? Were the rumors true? Or was the age difference too much? Who knows, but the new rumors are that he is dating another Hollywood actress.

▶ 9.5

P = principal   M = Michael

P Well Michael, you have a very interesting résumé and a lot of experience. Now we would like to ask some questions about classroom management, OK? Now the first question is: What would you do if the school caught fire?

M If the school caught fire? Oh, I would definitely run out of the classroom as quickly as possible. I don't want to get hurt!

P Oh, I see. OK, if your students were making too much noise, how would you control them?

M Oh, I wouldn't do anything. I would just wait for them to stop. If they were shouting for a long time, maybe I would read a book or something. I think it's important that students express themselves naturally in the classroom.

P Hmmm. OK, Michael. What would you do if there was a power outage?

M Ummm... I would probably send the students home. I can't teach if I don't have a computer.

P Hmm, OK. Now, the final question. If you were me, would you give yourself this job?

M Yes, of course I would. I'm a fantastic teacher.

57

Audioscript

▶9.10

M = man   W = woman

W Have you seen my glasses?

M Have you lost them again? Well, they could be in the living room. We were watching TV last night.

W No, they can't be in there. I'm sure I've had them today.

M Ummm, they might be in your bag. You often leave them in there.

W No, I've already checked.

M Well... they might be next to the computer. You were using the Internet earlier.

W No, I don't think they are there. I don't need my glasses for typing.

M Well, they must be somewhere. Have you looked in the car?

W Ah! You're right! They must be in there. I had them when I went to the store. I must be getting old!

▶9.13

M = man   W = woman

1 M1 I'm trying to sell my car.

  W1 What about putting an ad on the Internet?

2 M2 I had a big argument with my girlfriend and now we are not speaking.

  W2 If I were you, I'd call her.

3 W3 I'm so tired.

  M3 Why don't you go to bed?

4 W4 I'm really hungry, I haven't eaten since breakfast.

  M4 You'd better eat something.

5 M5 I'm a bit worried because I keep failing my exams.

  W5 You should study more often.

Unit 10

▶10.1

Let's start by finding out what stress is. So, stress is your body's way of reacting to situations around you. There are two main kinds of stress: acute, or sudden stress, and chronic stress. Acute stress is very common and it usually isn't dangerous to our health. It can be caused by short, positive experiences, such as excitement, getting married, starting a new job, or negative experiences, like rush hour traffic.

Umm, chronic stress is very different and it is always very unhealthy. It is caused by long experiences like, uh, unhappy relationships or poverty, uh, career problems or sickness.

Now, stress can have emotional or physical symptoms and, ummm, I'd like to talk about the physical side of stress.

So, first, when you get stressed your muscles tense, causing headaches and other muscle problems, and, aahh, this can make you feel very tired.

One interesting effect of acute stress is that your heart beats faster. This is why extreme sports are so exciting. However, if it happens too often, you may develop heart problems.

A lot of people feel tired when they get stressed, so they drink a lot of coffee to stay awake. Unfortunately, many scientists believe that caffeine increases the physical symptoms of stress, like your heart beating faster.

Another thing is diet. Stress can change the way you eat and can make you eat more than usual.

OK, and next, I'd like to talk about the emotional side of stress...

▶10.6

G = Gary   P = Pete

G I'm talking today to a big music fan, Pete.

P Hi Gary, well I'm a huge fan of Bruno Mars. He's an amazing singer and has been a superstar for years.

G That's right. Exactly how long has Bruno Mars been a singer?

P Fifteen years, and in that time he has had so many fantastic songs.

G How many number ones has he had?

P He's had seven! I mean, that is an incredible number. And he's won lots of awards.

G How many awards has he won?

P Nearly forty! And that includes eleven Grammy awards and four Guinness World records.

G Wow, that's amazing! Has he ever performed in South America?

P Yes he has. The largest concert was at Morumbi Stadium in São Paulo.

G How many people watched him there?

P Over 80,000 people went to see him play.

G Amazing. When did he perform in São Paulo?

P In 2017. That concert made a lot of money.

G I can imagine. How much money did the concert make, exactly?

P That concert alone made over six million dollars.

G Wow!

58

Answer Key

Unit 1

1.1

2 a education b Love c career d have fun
e free time f friends / family

3 b fitness a culture
d financial security c health

4 b, c, a, d

5 a cooked / took b watched c 're learning
d want / chose e doesn't cost f meet
g love / 'm really enjoying h went / 'm

6 Ad 1: f, h Ad 2: a, c Ad 3: b, g Ad 4: d, e

7 Personal answers.

1.2

1 1 great / bland 2 awesome / soft
3 fantastic / awful 4 sour / spicy, spicy / sour

2 a Look at / touch / watch / see
b smell / smells / taste / tastes / Eat
c feel / look / smells / listen to
d listen to / hear / sound / Read

3 The rhymes are:
1 store / more 2 breakfast / Texas ("Brenda,"
"bread," "breakfast" all have the same "br"
consonant sound) 3 machine / clean
4 fight / night ("rock" and "stop" have the same
vowel sound)

5 Personal answers.

1.3

1 will / will / won't / 'll / 'll

2 a She will probably take all of his money.
b Yinsen will die. c I will call and order some
pizza. d She will get married. e I will have the
vegetarian one. f Stark will definitely become a
superhero.

3 a P b P c U d P e U f P

4 Chris can't afford the pizza (b) and Rachel's pizza
is too big (d).

5 a I'll get it. (U)
b I'll go. (U)
c I won't eat. (P)
d I'll take it. (U)

6 Personal answers.

7 a bubbles b cozy c moist d leather
e countryside

1.4

1 Four reasons: feel stressed / have to care for your
children / went out late last night / it's a beautiful
sunny day and you just don't want to work.

2 a 3 Your time off c 2 Inform your boss
b 4 Going back to work d 1 Preparation

3 Personal answers.

4 a shouldn't b should c shouldn't
d shouldn't e shouldn't

6 /ʊ/ put, book, cook
/u:/ shoes, soup, two, true

7 Personal answers.

1.5

1 b (Netflix, etc.) e (Text messaging)
2 a yourself b – c yourself d – e –
3 1 a 2 b 3 c

---

4 b I'm going to wash the dishes. / Would you like
me to dry? / Yes, please. c These bags are really
heavy. / I'll carry one for you. / That's very kind of
you. d I don't understand this problem. / Do
you want a hand? / Yes, please. e It's really cold
in here. / Do you want me to turn off the A/C? /
Thanks for the offer but I can do it.

5 a Do you need a hand?
b Would you like me to help you?
c Do you want me turn off the music?
d Can I help you?

Unit 2

2.1

1 a TV b Newspapers c Internet d Today

2 a T b F c T

3 **in** the sports section, an article, a magazine
on the front page, a tablet, TV

4 a on Sundays b very interesting c sports
section d a magazine e waste of paper
f the Internet

5 a Yesterday's / was b look at / in
c waste / on d on e in f in

6 Personal answers.

2.2

1 a did you like b was watching c loved
d was talking e was playing

2 a Mother: Why were you fighting?
Sons: We **weren't fighting**. We **were playing**.
b Boss: Why weren't you working?
Employee: I **was sending** an email to a client.
c Angry girlfriend: Why was she texting you?
Boyfriend: She **was asking** for a friend's phone
number.
d Angry boyfriend: Why didn't you call me?
Girlfriend: Sorry, but my phone **wasn't working**.

4 1 She was asking for a friend's phone number.
2 We weren't fighting. We were playing.
3 Sorry, but my phone wasn't working.
4 I was sending an email to a client.

5 a wasn't eating / tasted b Did / taste
c Did / have d was having e Did / like
f wasn't listening

6 Personal answers.

2.3

1 a corruption b pollution c poverty
d crime e climate change f unemployment
g animal extinction h disease

2 a 200,000 b 200,000,000 c 1 d 13
e 30 f 2,800,000 g 3,200 h 88.2%
The extra number is 2,300.

3 a rainbow b eclipse c earthquake
d wildfire e hurricane f drought
g tsunami h flood i thunderstorm

4 a eclipse / were watching / earthquakes
b drought / weren't growing c flood / was
staying d was playing / thunderstorm /
lightning e was watching / hurricane / was
raining / rainbow

5 a cousins, double, trouble, mother
b about, house, clouds, thousand, down, loud,
found, town c would, good, Hollywood, should

---

6 Personal answers.

2.4

1 Story 1: a, b   Story 2: c, f   Story 3: d, e

2 a was working with / opened / walked
b was watching / heard
c was talking / offered

3 a didn't like
b were you doing / phoned
c was chatting / went out
d were you talking / came
e was walking / broke

4 a When I **was young** / **younger** I **played** a lot of
video games.
b My phone **rang** when I was in **the** middle of
taking a test at school.
c My friends **weren't** smiling when I **took** a
photo of them.
d What **were you** doing **last** night when the
outage happened?

5 a I was walking on the street when it started to
rain.
b I was working when there was a power outage.
c I was jogging in the park when a dog attacked
me.
d I was playing the piano when my cat jumped
on it.

6 Personal answers.

2.5

1
1	8
10	2
5	3
7	11
9	6
12	4

2 Personal answers.

3 a What happened? b Why was she on fire?
c The stones caught fire? d Is she OK?

4 c, a, e, d, b

Unit 3

3.1

1 2 pack your bags 3 take a taxi to the airport
4 board the plane 5 have a snack on the plane
6 stand in line 7 be stopped at customs
8 check in to your hotel

2 1 packed
2 arrived
3 missed
4 Book
5 broke down
6 hitchhiked
7 crowded
8 boarded

3 Person 1 on / on / on / on / in / on
Person 2 in / on / in / in / in
Person 3 a / the / the / the / the / the / – / The
/ – / the / The / –

4 a 3 b 2 and 3 c 2 d 1 e 2

5 a Do you get stressed when things go wrong?
b Did your last vacation go well?
c Do you get angry when you miss the bus?
d Do you get impatient with young kids on
planes?

60

Answer key

3.2

1

	This month	In the last 6 months	Never
books	✓		
music	✓		
movies	✓		
travel tickets			✓
hotel rooms			✓
event tickets		✓	
electronic equipment			✓
clothes			✓

2 b What have you bought online this month?
  c She has watched a movie online twice this month.
  d Have you ever booked a hotel online?
  e She has never booked travel tickets online.
  f She has gone shopping today.

3 Personal answers.

4 Personal answers.

5 a Where was the lake?
  b When did you wear it?
  c How often do you give money?
  d Did you speak to him or her?
  e What did it taste like?
  f Where did you plant it?
  g Did you go on vacation?
  h Can you teach me something?
  i How long did you fly for?

6 a Have you ever **swum** in a lake? No, but I **swam** in a river when I was on vacation.
  b The last time I **wore** a tie was when I was at **school**.
  c **Have** you ever **bought** clothes online?
  d Have you **ever been** abroad? Yes, I have been **to** Canada twice.

7 three, tree – a mean, seen, clean
  run, sun – b swum, money, done
  four, door – c board, orange, before

8 Personal answers.

3.3

1 a 3 b 1 c 2 d 4

2 a The dogsitter hasn't arrived **yet**.
  b I've **already** told you.
  c Have you fed the dog **yet**?
  d I've **already** bought some food for her.
  e I've **just** remembered!

3 a is b only c recently d before now
  e all prepared

4 b I've already / just gone online.
  I haven't gone online yet.
  c My friend has already / just called me.
  My friend hasn't called me yet.
  d I have already / just left home.
  I haven't left home yet.
  e I have already / just eaten dinner.
  I haven't eaten dinner yet.
  f I have already / just taken a shower.
  I haven't taken a shower yet.
  g I have already / just checked my e-mail.
  I haven't checked my e-mail yet.
  h I have already / just done a lot of exercise.
  I haven't done a lot of exercise yet.

5 1 **Basilica** – B (planned completion 2026-2028).
  2 **1,000 Trees** – B (planned completion 2020).
  3 **The Diamond** – A (planned but building won't start till 2023).
  4 **Costanera Center** – C.

3.4

1 c, e, d, a, b

2 e

3 a d b for / c c for / f d since / e
  e for / b f for / g g since / a

5 Personal answers.

3.5

1 have / had / has / be / is

2 1 convic**tion**s 2 corrobora**tion** 3 environ**ment**
  4 pre-histor**ic** 5 scientif**ic** 6 investiga**tion**
  7 equip**ment** 8 precis**ion** 9 argu**ment**
  10 loca**tion** 11 occasion**al**

3 3, 5, 6, 1, 4, 7

4 1 Wait a minute. 2 I'm sorry, I don't agree.
  3 What do you mean 4 You never told me

Unit 4

4.1

1 a Past b Infinitive

2 a bought b got c took d go e went f laughed

3 a F b T c F

4 Type A kind (11), sensitive (13), shy (14)
  Type B creative (3), curious (5), independent (9)
  Type AB critical (4), hardworking (7), honest (8), responsible (10), obedient (12)
  Type O active (1), aggressive (2), funny (6), sociable (15), spoiled (16)

5 Type A software engineer, librarian
  Type B cook, hair stylist, journalist
  Type AB lawyer, teacher
  Type O athlete, bank manager, politician

6 Personal answers.

4.2

1 a 4 b 6 c 1 d 3 e 7 f 2 g 5

2 Did you / love playing sports / what sport / when I was / did you do / used to go / didn't use to

4 d, c, a, b

5 a Who used to take you to school?
  b Which cartoons did you use to watch?
  c What food did you use to hate?

6 castle, Christmas, listen, often

4.3

1 Across
  1 records 5 pop 6 streaming 7 vinyl
  Down
  2 download 3 MP3s 4 turntable 5 punk

2 a PR b PA c PA d PR e B

3 1 b, f 2 a 3 d, g 4 e 5 c

4 Personal answers.

4.4

1 big / small   easy / difficult
  expensive / cheap heavy / light
  unclear / clear unpopular / popular

2 Type A big, clear, small, light, cheap
  Type B heavy, easy
  Type C popular, difficult, expensive, unclear, unpopular

3 c The Dall P45's memory is as big as the Star's.
  d The Dall P45's picture is clearer than the Eye-let Mini's.
  e The Dall P45 is not as easy to use as the Eye-let Mini.
  f The Eye-let Mini is about as big as the Dall P45.
  g The Dall P45 is the cheapest.

5 Personal answers.

4.5

1 4, 1, 3, 2

2 d – but e – so f – so b – but a – so c – but

3 a her nephew b 21 c $20 d money

4 b, d, a, c

5 c, e, b, a, d

6 a have b talk c buying d asking

Unit 5

5.1

1 biology, computer systems, economics, geography, literature, mathematics, physics, politics, psychology, sociology.
The hidden phrase is: "You get as much education outside school as in."

2 business, chemistry, engineering, languages, law

4 1 law 2 chemistry 3 business
  4 engineering 5 languages

5 a in b in c at d –

6 a Helen: Brinton, it's a long way from home, an attractive campus, bachelor's in business, the good teachers, make a million dollars a month.
  b Janet: Arleston, I can get here easily, babysitting facilities, vocational certificate in cooking, the evening classes, open a café.

7 Possible answer: Hi, I'm Leona and I study at Marlbury College. I chose this college because it has a great reputation and it's good because it has modern facilities. I'm doing a master's in chemistry and I really like it because of the excellent technology. One day, I want to develop new medicines.

8 Personal answers.

5.2

1 Tuesday: h, i Wednesday: d, f
Thursday: e, g Friday: a, j

2 Tuesday: literature Wednesday: economics
Thursday: physics Friday: mathematics
Extra subject: chemistry

3 a Why didn't Carrie talk about pollution? / Another student dominated the conversation.
  b What exercise did she enjoy on Tuesday? / The quiz.
  c How long does she have to write the paper? / One week.
  d What was bad about Thursday? / The pair work partner was a bit weird.

4 a can't b don't have to c can't d have to
  e can't f don't have to g don't have to
  h have to / don't have to

6 Personal answers.

5.3

1 a 3 b 4 c 5 d 2 e 1

2 a enough b too c Too / Too d enough / enough / enough

61

Answer Key

3 a We don't have enough gasoline. b There's been too much rain. c The shirt isn't big enough. d It's too far away. e There aren't enough boats. f The suitcase is too heavy for him. g The man is too weak to lift the suitcase. h He's eaten too much food.
1 c,h 2 f,g 3 b,e 4 a,d

4 b are / too / people c not / enough d don't / enough / money

5 /ʌ/ enough, fun, gum, someone, much, money /uː/ do, you, school, blue, chewing, food, you, who, too

6 Personal answers.

5.4

1 If I go to work, I'll meet my friends.
If I meet my friends, we'll go out.
If we go out, you'll get jealous.
If you get jealous, you'll divorce me.

2 c, a, b

3 b help c won't a take b is c are traveling

4 a Call them if you get lost / If you get lost, call them.
b If you travel by bus, sit close to the door. / Sit close to the door if you travel by bus.
c Don't be shy if someone talks to you! / If someone talks to you, don't be shy!
d Don't worry if you don't speak the language. / If you don't speak the language, don't worry.

5 b If you don't have a passport, you can't go abroad.
c If I take a vacation, I'll go to the beach.
d I feel sick if I eat too many cup cakes.
e If / When you travel, you learn new things.
f Your vacation will be great if it is sunny.
g What will you do if it snows?

7 Personal answers.

5.5

1 1 my 2 I 3 I 4 I 5 them 6 He 7 he 8 him 9 it 10 she 11 her 12 I 13 they 14 I 15 them 16 I 17 my 18 she 19 we 20 us 21 we

2 a F b N (We don't know if Anna replied or not.) c F d T e T

3 a 4 b 6 c 3 d 1 e 5 f 2

4 a Watch / make / a / noise b it'll / break c move / You / have d don't / forget / to e if / you / help / me f pass / your / exam

5 Personal answers.

6 c, b, e, a, d

Unit 6

6.1

2 a went camping b hang out, go clubbing c go diving d work out e go fishing, go bowling, climbing

3 a EZ and Angryman13. b Anya. c Sue and EZ. d Brad. e No, "climbing up the walls" means he is frustrated.

4 Personal answers.

6.2

1 Jillian, Frederico, Heitor

2 down / on / in / into

3 a gloves / hands b water level / unusually high c hiking / mountains

4 b port c room d paper e board f sun g hand h grand

5 a handshake b sandpaper c sunbathing d computer port

6 a dive b run c snowboard d jump e fall f swim g climb

7 Personal answers.

6.3

1 a towards / over / into / out of / under b across / up / past / down

2 a 4 b 3 c 7 d 6 e 1 f 2 g 5

3 Verbs: *adore* and *enjoy* = similar, positive meaning. *Adore* is stronger.
dislike and *can't stand* = similar, negative meaning. *Can't stand* is stronger.
Adjectives: *beautiful* is stronger than *pretty*; *huge* is stronger than *large*; *hilarious* is stronger than *funny*.
d, a, e, b, c

4 Possible answers:
b My mom dislikes cleaning the house.
c I adore going clubbing.
d My best friend can't stand shopping.
e I dislike traveling long distances.
f I enjoy working out.

5 1 /ð/ with, there, without, father, mother, brother, the
2 /θ/ threw, toothbrush, through
b It could be me, one of my siblings, or one of my cousins.

6.4

1 a scuba diving b through – swimming c over – volleyball d around – baseball e into – soccer

2 a mask, oxygen tank, fins b – c ball, net d bat, gloves e goal

3 interviewing / to be / working out / to help / to join / to learn / smoking / to quit / to make / to relax

5 a studying b to study c to study d to study e to study f studying

6.5

1 a bull b horns c crowd

2 Shane has run with the bulls.

3 4, 1, 2, 3

4 a 5, 2, 3, 4, 1 b 3, 6, 1, 5, 4, 2

5 a prefers listening / quieter bands b would love / see them

Unit 7

7.1

1 a sequel b stunt c box office d review e subtitles f plot g soundtrack

2 a mystery b drama c animated d action e thriller f documentary g horror h adventure i comedy j fantasy

3 1 Comedy – a 2 Suspense – c 3 Gangster – b

4 a 1 b 2 c 2 d 3 e 1

5 a *Terminator 2* is **an** old movie...
b **Most** actors want to win **an** Oscar.
c I watched a great movie on **TV last night**.

6 Personal answers.

7.2

1 a into b crazy c obsessed d huge fans

2 a photo (the photo doesn't move) b haircut (you can't take it off) c general public (paparazzi and journalist are media jobs) d huge (an adjective – it means very / really big) e obsessed (an adjective, needs a preposition "with")

3 a nothing b anyone c something d everybody / nobody e someone f anywhere

4 nothing / no one / anything / anywhere / someone / anyone's / everyone / somewhere / everywhere / nowhere / Everything / something / Everyone

5 a no b fan c one

6 Personal answers.

7.3

1 d 1 c 2 a 3 b 4

2 1 such an 2 so 3 so 4 so 5 such a 6 such a 7 so 8 so

4 a Do you b Are you c Do you / a d do you

5 a How many – About 50.
b How often – About once a week.
c Have you ever – Unfortunately, no, I haven't.
d been to a game – Yeah, I went last year.

7.4

1 b

2 These verb forms must be **crossed out**: is released / create / is gotten / didn't intend / were persuaded / captures / is made / accidently throw / are found / joined

3 a 1.9 billion b 99.7 c one and a half d third / 14 e two fifths f 21st / twenty-first

4 a *Game of Thrones* was written by George R.R. Martin. (I)
b "Live it up", the official song of the 2018 World Cup, was sung by Nicky Jam featuring Will Smith and Era Istrefi. (I)
c The World Wide Web was invented by Tim Berners-Lee. (R)
d Microsoft was founded by Bill Gates and Paul Allen. (R)

5 b 1 c 1 d 2 e 2 f 1

6 Personal answers.

7.5

1

/ʃ/ shorts	/tʃ/ cheese	/ʒ/ treasure
ex**pres**sion, partici**pa**tion, po**si**tion, pronun**cia**tion, **sh**ow	**catch**, **church**, **kitch**en, **ques**tion	con**clu**sion, de**ci**sion, il**lu**sion,

2 Check answers in 1. The syllable before -ion is stressed.

3 a What is Jess watching on TV? (Big Brother.)
b Does Helen like the show? (No.)

62

Answer Key

c Why does Helen feel nervous? (Because she has an interview.)

4 1, 2, 3

5 a It / good / I expected b I / think it was
c It was

6 Personal answers.

7 e, d, a, b, c

8 a It was such a noisy place.
b I have such a slow car.
c It was such a disappointing movie/ disappointment.
d It was such an interesting documentary.
e It is such a popular radio station.
f She has such a strange collection of chairs.

Unit 8

8.1

1 a at / on b in c at / on d in

2 a a smell-producing alarm clock b a self-heating lunch box c a news-summarizing app

3 a F b N c T d N e F

4 a 2 b 6 c 1 d 4 e 7 f 3 g 5

5 a vending b GPS c speaker d lenses
e facial

6 Personal answers.

8.2

1 a connect to electricity
b disconnect using a switch
c make quieter
d stop sleeping
e get out of bed in the morning
f make louder
g make a machine start working

2 a 2 b 4 c 1 d 3

4 1 on / off button 2 USB cable
3 volume icon   on / off / up / down / up

5 a Is that your new cell phone? ↗
b Where did you buy it? ↘
c How long does the battery last? ↘
d Can I play with it? ↗
e How many apps do you have? ↘
f What does this app do? ↗

6 Personal answers.

8.3

1

/θ/	/ð/
synthetic, telepathy, think, thirty, thoughts, three, through	the, themselves, there, they, this

2 b We will **probably** be able to... / ... and will **possibly** have celebrity... c There have **certainly** been big... / ... this will **certainly** continue. d ... organizations will **possibly** use... e We **probably** won't use cell... / ... we will **possibly** be able to...

3 b Cell phones will possibly be able to clean themselves. c Cell phones definitely won't be "phones." d We probably won't need to touch the screens. e Cell phones will certainly be able to recognize our voices.

4 a **Will** 3D TV be common in five years?
b Will **there be** a World War 3? c Did we **have** homework from the last class? d Are we **going** to have a test this week? e Is **it** going to

be sunny this weekend? f Will we be able to **communicate** with aliens one day?

5 b I hope not. It would be terrible! c I think so. But I can't remember. d I hope not. I think it's next week. e I think so. They said it will be.
f I hope so. They are usually cool in the movies!

7 Personal answers.

8.4

1 b arguments c answer d take place
e take f sensitive g intends

2 b assume c sensible d pretended / was pretending e realized f actually g attend

3 finish, leaves, going to have to, 'll ask / 'm going to ask, 'm staying, 's going to be / will be

4 a I will b I'll c He's going to
d isn't going to e I'll

5 a What time does your next lesson start?
b What are you doing this weekend? / What are you going to do this weekend?
c Do you think we will stop driving cars in the future?
d Are you going to do any homework tomorrow?

8.5

1 a give b hour c busy

2 Suggested answers.
a Bike for sale. Five years old. Very good condition. $80.
b Waiter needed. Busy city center restaurant. Experience required. Good pay.
c Babysitting service offered. Weekdays only. $10 per hour. Call 733-383-6876.

3 1 b 2 c 3 b 4 a

5 c, a, e, d, b

Unit 9

9.1

1 engagement, honeymoon, ceremony, guest list, gift registry, invitation, reception, bride, groom, bridesmaids

2 a 2 (Evelyn Hendrickson) b 5 (Billy Connolly)
c 1 (Henry Youngman) d 3 (Albert Einstein)
e 4 (Rodney Dangerfield)

3 a get dark b get lost c get better
d get wet e get dressed

4 a F b T c F d F e N f F g T

5 a Jessica Biel got married to Justin Timberlake in 2012.
b Mark Zuckerberg married Priscilla Chan in their garden.
c Michael Bublé got married to Luisana Lopilato in Vancouver and Buenos Aires.

6 Personal answers.

9.2

1 Sep. 13 – bored / tired / amazing / funny
Sep. 14 – terrifying / surprised / scared / exciting
Sep. 15 – interested / satisfied / "entertaining"

2 a classes b teacher c doesn't like d liked

3 a exciting b tired c surprising
d irritated e terrifying

4 completely, extremely, really, very, totally; "absolutely", "completely", "totally" have the same meaning.

5 Personal answers.

6

1 syllable	2 syllables	3 syllables
broke, dumped, fell	cheated, dated, flirted	attracted

"Break" and "fall" are irregular.

7 1 attracted 2 fell 3 cheated 4 flirted
5 break up 6 dump 7 dating

8 1 After 6 years, Demi decided to break up with Ashton. 2 Demi is 16 years older than Ashton. 3 They met in 2003. 4 They got married in 2005.
The extra number is 60.

9.3

1 a the school caught fire b were making too much noise c What would you do d If you were me

2 a I wouldn't do anything. – b b Yes, of course I would. – d c I would definitely run out of the classroom. – a d I would probably send the students home. – c

3 a If you were the interviewer, would you give Mike the job?
b If you were the teacher, what would you do next class?
c If you could travel anywhere, where would you go?
d How would you feel if you lost your cell phone?
e If you had a million dollars, what would you spend it on?

4 e, b, a, d, g, c, f

5 a **g**eography 2   **j**ournal 2
b **j**ealous 2   **ed**itor 1
c **id**ea 1   marria**g**e 2
d e**dg**e 2   **d**iary 1
e **g**enuinely 2   **d**ifferent 1

9.4

1 b ath-lete   f ce-leb-ri-ty
c co-me-di-an   g run-ner
d gui-tar-ist   h ma-gi-cian
e gym-nast

2 She has lost her glasses. She says "I must be getting old" because she keeps forgetting things.

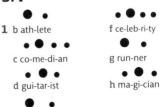

63

Answer Key

3

Location that the man suggests	Reason	✓ or ✗	Reason
living room	**Watching TV last night.**	✗	**Sure she has had them today.**
in her bag	She often leaves her glasses there.	✗	**She has already checked.**
next to the computer	**She was using the Internet earlier.**	✗	She doesn't need them for typing.
in the car	They must be somewhere.	✓	**She had them when she went to the shop.**

4 b 4 c 6 d 1 e 2 f 5
Pictures 1 d, 2 e, 3 b.

5 Personal answers.

6 Personal answers.

9.5

1 a N b F c T d T e F f N

2 They / them / their / They / them / them / Their / they / them / they / their / Their

3 a Why **don't** you go to bed?
b If I **were** you, I'd call her.
c **You** should study more often.
d What **about** putting an ad on the Internet?
e You**'d** better eat something.

4 1 d 2 b 3 a 4 e 5 c

Unit 10

10.1

1 a an expert on stress
b two
c both positive and negative
d always
e physical

2 a married b traffic c relationships d career
e headaches f Acute g physical h more

3 a C b C c A d A e C

4 a undercooked b overpaid c overeat
d overspent e underestimated

10.2

1 a That's a **bad** cough. Why don't you quit **smoking**?
b Ugh! Your cooking is so salty. You should **use less** salt.
c I'm not going **to** lend you any money so you'd better **spend** less.
d You don't play any sports and you drive everywhere. Why **don't** you **exercise** more?
e You won't pass your school test if you don't study more and **watch less** TV.

3 Across
3 hotel 5 that – racket 7 who – judge (d)
9 who – bridesmaids (f) 10 that – Las Vegas
12 that – church
Down
1 that – box office (a) 2 who – fortune-teller (b)
4 who – lifeguard 6 that – tent (c)
8 who – groom (e) 11 that – gym

4 a A place that lends books.
b A thing that you use to clean your house.
c A person who constructs new houses.

5 a Library b Vacuum cleaner c Builder

6 Personal answers.

10.3

1 Correct order: b, c, a.
afford / costs / earn / spend / pay for

2 a Earn Money b Win Money c Bargain
d Save Your Money e Lend Your Money

3 a It can be boring.
b You will almost certainly lose.
c This can be a little embarrassing.
d It will be a very long time before you are rich.
e This can be a risky way to get rich.

4 abandoned / those things / take / pick it up / carry / house / excited

10.4

1 a How long has Bruno been a singer?
b How many number-one singles has he had?
c How many awards has he won?
d How many people watched him in São Paulo?
e When did he perform in São Paulo?
f How much money did the concert make?

2 a 15 b seven c 40 d 80,000
e 2017 f 6 million

3 1 b
2 What event did Charlie do? b
3 Which soccer team does Jason love? c
4 What does Barbara collect? b
5 How many jobs are lost because of illegal downloads? c
6 What music did the guy request in lesson 8.1? a
7 According to Penny Duff, how will we communicate in the future? a
8 What does Matt Jones offer help with? b
9 How high is a "Marriage in the Sky"? c
10 How many countries do they operate in? b

4 1 /ʃ/ **sh**ark, **sh**orts, consump**ti**on, conven**ti**onal, participa**ti**on
2 /ʒ/ televi**si**on, trea**sure**, deci**si**on, lei**sure**, occa**si**on

10.5

1 1 It's a school.
2 Because he went to school with them.
3 Because he was wearing an expensive suit.
4 Jed – big hands.
5 Marcus feels angry.
6 He put something in it.

4 a Which **ones** would you like to try? / I like the black **ones** in the window.
The **one** next to the movie theater.
b Yes, we have purple **ones** and green **ones**. Which **ones** would you like?
c Yes. This **one** has a good map and this **one** has lots of historical information.
I'll have the **one** with the map, please.

Phrase Bank

This Phrase Bank is organized by topics.
▶ The audio is on the **ID** Richmond Learning Platform.

Offering help

Unit 1
Do you want me to drive?
Don't worry. This course doesn't cost anything.
Can I help you?
Do you need a hand?
Would you like me to help you?
Yes, please! That's very kind of you!
Thanks for the offer.

About you

Unit 1
My name's Arturo Hernandez and I'm a web designer.
What do you do to stay in shape?
I'm careful about my diet and do a lot of exercise.
I always need a partner.
I never stop studying.
I'd love to work in the movie industry.
I'm planning to live to be 100.

Unit 3
You have no idea how shy I am.

Expressing opinions, agreeing and disagreeing

Unit 3
I think it's very important to compromise.
No way!

Unit 4
I disagree.
In my opinion, CDs are the highest quality music.
I think it's better to study from home, because you can save a lot of money. But you don't have friends to talk to.
I'm not sure I agree with you.

Unit 5
For me, it's important to have great teachers.
Evening classes aren't important for me.

Unit 6
I guess bowling is usually safe.

Unit 7
I'm not sure if he's crying or sweating. What do you think?
I think if they make downloading cheaper, there will be less piracy.
I think most men enjoy action movies.
Actually, I didn't think Joe was that great.
I have to agree with Alice.
It wasn't as good as I expected.
I thought it was OK.

Unit 8
Do you think robots will replace teachers?
Oh really? I don't - I prefer to use my fingerprint.
Yeah. I hope so.
Oh, I hope not.
I don't think machines will ever feel anything.

Unit 8
I disagree.
Really? I don't think we'll change.
No, not a chance!

Unit 9
Weddings are boring 'cause they're always the same.
People usually fall in love with someone they find physically attractive.

Making comparisons

Unit 1
People are more important than things.
Time to enjoy things is more important than money.

Unit 4
Cats are not as good with kids as dogs are.
He looks funnier than the other guy.
A tablet is as useful as a laptop.
LPs are better than CDs.

Making guesses

Unit 1
I think she's going to be late.

Unit 8
Maybe machines will have human emotions.
Ten years from now, there will probably be house-cleaning robots.
Well, I don't think the Internet will change much.
Yeah, I doubt it. But we'll find different ways to use it.

Unit 9
He must be a celebrity.
It can't be a pear, because of the texture.
It might be an apple, because of the color.
Do you think they're German?

Unit 10
It could be about an old lady that decides to leave her home.

Phrase Bank

Making suggestions

Unit 1
You should take a painkiller.

Unit 4
Have you considered getting a fish?
Have you thought about getting a cat?
Why don't you get a small dog?
You should definitely get her a pet.

Unit 6
Let's go clubbing.

Unit 10
She should definitely buy a raffle ticket.
She needs to eat more—she looks really thin.

Memories

Unit 1
It reminds me of a band my brother was in.

Unit 3
That reminds me of my grandma's birthday party.

Unit 4
Did you use to make fun of other kids?
I think I was four or five.
I had a cat. It used to sleep in the sink.
I learned how to drive when I was 18 years old.
When did you get your first pet?
When I was young I had to wash the car every week.

Unit 6
I don't remember the last time we went to the beach.

Unit 9
The last time I was absolutely exhausted was after going clubbing.

Money

Unit 1
Can you lend me some money?
Can I borrow some money?

Unit 10
I have 50 dollars, but I want to save the money.
If I get another job, I can earn more money.

Talking about preferences

Unit 1
I enjoy working out.
I enjoy having fun.

Unit 2
I prefer real life so I'd watch the show about the jungle.
I'd like to watch that movie because I love horror.

Unit 6
Do you feel like going out?
I'd rather stay in.
I'd prefer to stay in.
I can't stand swimming.
I'd like to go to New York.
My favorite outdoor activities are swimming and hiking.
We adore playing basketball.
Would you rather eat Italian or Mexican food?

Talking about problems

Unit 1
Are you OK?
How are you feeling?
What's the matter?
I have a cold.
I missed a class and I have a test and I'm really worried.
If you have a cold, you shouldn't go to class.
My head hurts.
When you take an aspirin, you'll feel better.

Unit 2
I think pollution affects oceans, lakes, rivers, and cities.
I think crime is the most serious problem here.

Unit 10
Lack of sleep is a problem for me.

Defining language

Unit 1
Bland means "without taste".

Unit 2
It's the opposite of easy.
It's like the world, but bigger.

Describing events

Unit 2
I was cooking dinner when the lights went out.
Jane was chatting online and her phone rang.
What were you doing when the outage happened?

Reacting to something negative

Unit 2
That's awful!
No way!
Oh no!
That's terrible!

67

Phrase Bank

Reacting to something positive

Unit 2
How interesting!
That's good.
That's great!
Wow! Really?

Showing you are listening

Unit 2
And then what happened?
Uh-huh?
Yes?

Talking about news

Unit 2
That's an important piece of news.
Last night's news was shocking.

Talking about TV

Unit 2
Did you see the show last night?
What was it about?
I was watching a show about climate change.

Showing desire

Unit 3
All I want to do is get some sleep.
All I wanted was to get some cash.
I really want to go to Europe.

Unit 8
I'd love to have a self-driving car.

Unit 10
I'd like to exercise more and eat better.

Showing surprise

Unit 3
But that makes no sense!
Oh, come on!
Wait a second. Did I hear you say that you wrote a song?
What do you mean, nothing?
You're kidding me!
You've never told me that!

Talking about completion

Unit 3
Have you done your homework yet?
I haven't done it yet.
I've already had breakfast.
I've just finished it.

Talking about duration

Unit 3
How long have you been in the UK?
Since last September.

Traveling

Unit 3
Did you go on business?
Have you ever seen the Statue of Liberty?
Yeah, twice.
Really? When did you go to New York?
I don't mind traveling long distances by car. I find it relaxing.
I haven't been abroad yet, but I'm going to Miami next year.
I'd love to take a year off and travel around India.
I've been abroad, but only once.
Oh really? Where did you go?
Oh yeah? Did you go on business?

Promises

Unit 5
If you eat all your dinner, I'll give you some ice cream.
If you finish your homework, I'll take you to the movies.
If you stay late, I'll give you the day off tomorrow.

School and education

Unit 5
A bad point about my school is that classes are really big.
I can't come to class tomorrow.
I chose English because I've always loved reading.
I have a vocational certificate in accounting.
I want to learn a language so I can get a better job.
I was interested in math because I was really good at it.
Why did you choose to study at this school?

Warning

Unit 5
Be careful!
Don't move!
I won't buy you a new bike if you don't get good grades.
Look out!
Watch out!
Whatever you do, don't eat that ice cream. If you do, you'll have to go to your room!
You'd better (not) do that!

Other useful expressions

Unit 1
I can't hear you.
I don't want to live in a world without culture.
I'll take your order now.
He will never amount to anything.
There's no chance that people will stop using the Internet.

68

Phrase Bank

Unit 3
I'm not going to waste my time taking a gap year.
In this situation, I shout until I get what I want.
It depends on how much.

Sports

Unit 6
You have to kick the ball into the goal.
You play the game with a bat and a ball.

Movies

Unit 7
My favorite movie is *The Green Book*.
I've never seen *The Artist*.
It has a superb plot and character and it's based on a true story.
For action, how about *Spiderman: Far From Home*?
Did it have good reviews?
Would you recommend it?
Who's the main character?

Being a fan

Unit 7
I'm really into plants and I have my own garden.
I'm obsessed with Manchester United.
I'm really into sport.
I'm crazy about music.
I'm a big fan of getting involved with campaigns.

Pausing

Unit 7
Anyway, the big day arrived and I got there early.
Where was I?

Predictions

Unit 8
Am I going to marry my boyfriend?
Probably. / There's a good chance.
Definitely. / For sure. / Absolutely.
Are we ever going to travel through time?
Will we have house-cleaning robots?
Probably not. / I doubt it.
Definitely not. / Not a chance. / No way.

Giving advice and responding

Unit 9
If I were you, I'd talk to your boss.
Thanks for the tip. I hadn't thought of that.
What about calling my brother?
Why don't you go to the mall?
I'd find out how Juan feels.
Thanks for the suggestion, but I don't have time now.
You should go home and go to bed.
You're right.
You'd better start working harder.
That's a good idea.
Yeah, I guess so.

Describing people and things

Unit 10
This is my sister Jane, who lives in L.A.
This is the hotel that we stayed in.

Other useful expressions

Unit 8
Why on Earth did she decide she should wake me up early?

Word List

Unit 1

Life priorities
career
culture
education
family
financial security
fitness
free time
friends
having fun
health
love

The senses
to eat
to hear
hearing
to listen
to look
to see
sight
smell
to smell
to stink
taste
to taste
touch
to touch
to watch

Adjectives
amazing
awesome
awful
bland
cool
cozy
delicious
fresh
loud
moist
quiet
rotten
rough
salty
smoky
soft
sour
spicy
spongy
stylish
sweet
terrible

Common illnesses
backache
a cold
a cough
earache
a fever
the flu
a headache
stomachache
toothache

Other words
bathtime
bubbles
collar
countryside
leather
pocket

Unit 2

News
business news
celebrity gossip
entertainment
local / national news
in a newspaper
in the headlines
on a mobile device
on a news website or app
on a screen
on a smartphone
on social media
on the radio
on TV
world news

Global problems
animal extinction
climate change
corruption
crime
disease
global warming
pollution
poverty
unemployment

Geography
cities
deserts
jungles
lakes
oceans
rainforests
rivers
wildlife

Natural phenomena
drought
earthquake
eclipse
flood
high waves
hurricane
lightning
rainbow
thunderstorm
tsunami

Other words
fraud
habitat
huge
to investigate
overated
power outage
rocks
shocking
to survive
totality
uneasy
universe

Unit 3

Traveling
to board a plane
to book a hotel
crowded station
customs
day trip
to hitchhike
to miss a train
to pack your bags
to stand in line

Ambitions
to be a DJ
to do volunteer work
to donate blood
to fall in love
to go abroad
to have a child
to learn to dance
to make a cake
to plant a tree
to ride an animal
to swim with dolphins
to try an extreme sport
to visit London
to write a story

Other words
amenities
basic
cleanliness
disappointment
dramatic
emotionally
equipment
information
intellectual
mental
moon
musical
renovation
resort
romantic
typical

Unit 4

Adjectives
active
aggressive
creative
critical
curious
funny
hardworking
honest
independent
kind
lazy
obedient
responsible
sensitive
shy
sociable
spoiled

Do / Make
to do a favor
to do a project
to do activities
to do chores
to do homework
to do the dishes
to do the laundry
to do well
to make a decision
to make a mistake
to make a noise
to make a promise
to make an effort
to make contact
to make friends
to make fun of someone
to make money
to make the bed

Other words
to bark
to bite
kitten
to laugh
puppy
to scratch
sink

Unit 5

School subjects
art
biology
business
chemistry
computer systems
economics
engineering
geography
history
languages
law
literature
mathematics
physics
politics
psychology
sociology

In college
administrator
bachelor's degree
campus
evening class
facilities
lecture
master's degree
teacher
vocational education

Class activities
exam
group work activity
homework
journal entry
online practice
pair work activity
project
research
summary
test

Word List

Phrasal verbs

to catch up
to drop out of something
to find out

Unit 6

Leisure time activities

to go bowling
to go camping
to go climbing
to go clubbing
to go diving
to go fishing
to go hiking
to hang out
to work out

Verbs of movement

to climb
to fall
to fly
to get
to jump
to run
to snowboard
to swim

Compound nouns

hairbrush
lunchbox
mailbox
toothbrush

Prepositions of movement

across
along
around
down
into
out of
over
past
through
towards
under
up

Sports equipment

bat
fins
gloves
hoop
helmet
mask
net
puck
racket
snorkel
stick

Sports verbs

to catch
to hit
to kick
to shoot

Other words

harness
secure
to scream
to shake

Unit 7

Movie words

main character
to dub
to play someone
plot
review
scary
sequel
soundtrack
to star in
subtitles

Movie genres

action
adventure
animated
comedy
documentary
drama
horror
mystery
thriller

Unit 8

Technology

active contact lens
button
facial recognition device
speaker
surveillance camera
vending machine

Phrasal verbs

to get up
to plug in
to switch off
to switch on
to turn down
to turn up
to wake up

Unit 9

Marriage

bride
bridesmaid
ceremony
decorations
engagement party
gift registry
groom
guest list
honeymoon
reception
wedding invitation

Adjectives

amazed
amazing
bored
boring
confused
confusing
depressed
depressing
embarrassed
embarrassing
entertained
entertaining
excited

exciting
exhausted
exhausting
frightened
frightening
interested
interesting
irritated
irritating
relaxed
relaxing
satisfied
satisfying
scared
scary
stressed
stressful
surprised
surprising
terrified
terrifying
tired
tiring

Romance

to be attracted
to be in love with someone
to break up
to cheat
to date
to dump
to fall in love with someone
to have a crush on someone

Performers

actor
athlete
clown
comedian
dancer
gymnast
magician
musician
singer
skater

Characteristics

adaptable
charming
friendly
intelligent
irresponsible
mature

Unit 10

Causes and symptoms of stress

caring for a child
deadlines
financial problems
lack of exercise
lack of sleep
multitasking
peer pressure
poor diet
pressure to succeed

Relieving stress

to breathe deeply
to eat well
to exercise
to go clubbing
to have realistic deadlines
meditation

to plan your time
to relax
to sleep well
to spend time with friends
to take a break
to take medicine

Lifestyle changes

to drink less soda
to eat better
to eat less salt
to exercise more
to get a new job
to get more sleep
to lose weight
to organize and plan time
to spend less time online
to watch less TV
to work from home
to work less

Money verbs

to be able to afford
to cost
to earn
to pay
to save
to spend
to waste
to win

![Richmond]

Richmond

58 St Aldates
Oxford
OX1 1ST
United Kingdom

© Richmond / Santillana Global S.L. 2020

Second reprint: September 2020
ISBN: 978-84-668-3058-4
CP: 944439

All rights reserved. No part of this book may be reproduced, stored in a retrieval system or transmitted in any form by any means, electronic, mechanical, photocopying, recording or otherwise, without the prior permission in writing of the Publisher.

Publishing Director: Deborah Tricker
Publisher: Luke Baxter
Media Publisher: Luke Baxter
Managing Editor: Laura Miranda
Content development: Paul Seligson, Damian Williams
Editor: Sarah Curtis
Proofreaders: Cathy Heritage, Diyan Leake
Design Manager: Lorna Heaslip
Cover Design: Lorna Heaslip
Design & Layout: Dave Kuzmicki
Photo Researcher: Victoria Gaunt, Emily Taylor (Bobtail Media)
Audio Production: John Marshall Media Inc.

We would like to thank all those who have given their kind permission to reproduce material for this book:

Illustrators: Alexandre Matos, Rico, Leo Teixeira
Photos:
ALAMY STOCK PHOTO/AGB Photo Library, CHROMORANGE/Herwig Czizek, Diego Grandi, imageBROKER, JN, Mile Atanasov, MNStudio, Montgomery Martin, Minden Pictures; CARTOONSTOCK/Carroll Zahn; GETTY IMAGES SALES SPAIN/aedkais, Ariel Skelley, Beyond foto, Brand X, BrianAJackson,

Printers: PlenaPrint
Lot: 291728

Busà Photography, Caiaimage/Martin Barraud, Carol Grant, Chesky_W, Colin Anderson Productions pty ltd, Copyright Rhinoneal, Corbis, CreativeDJ, Cultura RF, Digital Vision, dmbaker, Drazen_, E+, Erik Isakson/Blend Images LLC, Erikreis, EyeEm, FotoSpeedy, FilmMagic, franckreporter, Fuse, Getty Images AsiaPac, Getty Images North America, George Pimentel, Geri Lavrov, gionnixxx, GlobalP, Hero Images, Huronphoto, Image Source, iStock Editorial, istockphoto, jcrosemann, Jeff Kravitz, Jerod Harris, Jekaterina Nikitina, Juanmonino, Jupiterimages, Jurgenfr, Karl-Friedrich Hohl, Kent Weakley, Kinemero, Michael J Cohen, Mipan, Mint Images RF, Obak, Klaus Vedfelt, oneword, ppa5, Peter Parks, Photo by Brook Rieman, Picture Press RM, Predrag Vuckovic, Roy Hsu, Sergeyryzhov, shapecharge, SolisImages, sturti, Taxi, The Image Bank, Timothy Norris, www.peopleimages.com; LUNCHEAZE; PLAINPICTURE/Jasmin Sander; SHUTTERSTOCK/Anitasstudio, Chiang Ying-Ying/AP, Dmitry Rukhlenko, egd, Gladskikh Tatiana, Hugo Felix, Inxti, Jenny Goodall/Daily Mail, kwanchai.c, Lineicons freebird, Marvel/Paramount/Kobal, Monkey Business Images, Nomad_Soul, Nina Anna, Radu Bercan, Ted Shaffrey/AP, Topseller, Zkruger; ARCHIVO SANTILLANA.

The Publisher has made every effort to trace the owner of copyright material; however, the Publisher will correct any involuntary omission at the earliest opportunity.

Printed in Brazil